# Safeguarding Equipment and Protecting Employees from Amputations

**Occupational Safety and Health Administration
U.S. Department of Labor**

OSHA 3170-02R
2007

# Contents

## List of Tables

## List of Figures

# Introduction

Amputations are among the most severe and disabling workplace injuries that often result in permanent disability. They are widespread and involve various activities and equipment. (The U.S. Bureau of Labor Statistics 2005 annual survey data indicated that there were 8,450 non-fatal amputation cases – involving days away from work – for all private industry. Approximately forty-four percent (44%) of all workplace amputations occurred in the manufacturing sector and the rest occurred across the construction, agriculture, wholesale and retail trade, and service industries.) These injuries result from the use and care of machines such as saws, presses, conveyors, and bending, rolling or shaping machines as well as from powered and non-powered hand tools, forklifts, doors, trash compactors and during materials handling activities.

Anyone responsible for the operation, servicing, and maintenance (also known as use and care) of machines (which, for purposes of this publication includes equipment) — employers, employees, safety professionals, and industrial hygienists— should read this publication. Primary safeguarding, as used in this publication, includes control methods that protect (e.g., prevent employee contact with hazardous machine areas) employees from machine hazards through effective machine guarding techniques. In addition, a hazardous energy control (lockout/tagout) program needs to complement machine safeguarding methods in order to protect employees during potentially hazardous servicing and maintenance work activities.

This guide can help you, the small business employer, identify and manage common amputation hazards associated with the operation and care of machines. The first two sections of the document, *Recognizing Amputation Hazards* and *Controlling Amputation Hazards*, look at sources of amputations and how to safeguard machinery and control employee exposure to hazardous energy (lockout/tagout) during machine servicing and maintenance activities. The section on *Specific Machinery Hazards and Safeguarding Methods* identifies the hazards and various control methods for machinery associated with workplace amputations, such as: mechanical power presses, press brakes, conveyors, printing presses, roll-forming and roll-bending machines, shears, food slicers, meat grinders, meat-cutting band saws, drill presses, milling machines, grinding machines, and slitting machines.

The information in this booklet does not specifically address amputation hazards on all types of machinery in general industry, construction, maritime and agricultural operations; however, many of the described safeguarding techniques may be used to prevent other amputation injuries. Additionally, while this manual concentrates attention on concepts and techniques for safeguarding mechanical motion, machines obviously present a variety of other types of energy hazards that cannot be ignored. For example, pressure system failure could cause fires and explosions. Machine electrical sources also pose electrical hazards that are addressed by other OSHA standards, such as the electrical standards contained in Subpart S. Full discussion of these matters is beyond the scope of this publication. For compliance assistance purposes, references and the appendices are provided on applicable OSHA standards, additional information sources, and ways you may obtain OSHA assistance.

## OSHA Standards

Although this guide recommends ways to safeguard and lockout/tagout energy sources associated with machinery hazards, there are legal requirements in OSHA standards that you need to know about and comply with. The following OSHA standards are a few of the regulations that protect employees from amputation hazards.

---

**Machinery and Machine Guarding:
29 CFR Part 1910, Subpart O**

- 1910.211 – *Definitions*
- 1910.212 – *General requirements for all machines*
- 1910.213 – *Woodworking machinery requirements*
- 1910.215 – *Abrasive wheel machinery*
- 1910.216 – *Mills and calenders in the rubber and plastics industries*
- 1910.217 – *Mechanical power presses*
- 1910.218 – *Forging machines*
- 1910.219 – *Mechanical power-transmission apparatus*

**Control of Hazardous Energy (Lockout/Tagout):
29 CFR 1910.147**

**Hand and Power Tools:
29 CFR Part 1926, Subpart I**

- 1926.300 – *General requirements*
- 1926.303 – *Abrasive wheels and tools*
- 1926.307 – *Mechanical power-transmission apparatus*

**Conveyors:
29 CFR 1926.555**

---

Consult these standards directly to ensure full compliance with the provisions as this publication is not a substitute for the standards. States with OSHA-approved plans have at least equivalent standards. For detailed information about machine guarding and lockout/tagout, see the following resources:

- Machine Guarding Safety and Health Topics Page (http://www.osha.gov/SLTC/machine guarding/index.html)
- Machine Guarding eTool (http://www.osha.gov/ SLTC/etools/machineguarding/index.html)
- OSHA Publication 3067, Concepts and Techniques of Machine Safeguarding (http://www.osha.gov/ Publications/Mach_Safeguarding/toc.html)
- OSHA Directive STD 01-05-019 [STD 1-7.3], Control of Hazardous Energy (Lockout/Tagout)— Inspection Procedures and Interpretive Guidance
- Control of Hazardous Energy (Lockout/Tagout) Safety and Health Topics Page (http://www.osha. gov/SLTC/controlhazardousenergy/index.html)
- OSHA's Lockout Tagout Interactive Training Program (http://www.osha.gov/dts/osta/ lototraining/index.htm)
- OSHA Publication 3120, Control of Hazardous Energy (Lockout/Tagout)

OSHA standards, directives, publications, and other resources are available online at www.osha.gov.

## National Consensus Standards

OSHA recognizes the valuable contributions of national consensus standards and these voluntary standards may be used as guidance and recognition of industry accepted practices. For example, the American National Standards Institute (ANSI) publishes numerous voluntary national consensus standards on the safe care and use of specific machinery. These consensus standards provide you with useful guidance on how to protect your em-ployees from machine amputation hazards and the control methods described may assist you in complying with OSHA performance-based standards.

Furthermore, OSHA encourages employers to abide by the more current industry consensus standards since those standards are more likely to be abreast of the state of the art than an applicable OSHA standard may be. However, when a consensus standard addresses safety considerations, OSHA may determine that the safety practices described by that consensus standard are less protective than the requirement(s) set forth by the pertinent OSHA regulations. OSHA enforcement policy regarding the use of consensus standards is that a violation of an OSHA standard may be deemed *de minimis* in nature if the employer complies with a consensus standard (that is not incorporated by reference) rather than the OSHA standard in effect and if the employer's action clearly provides equal or greater employee protection. (Such *de minimis* violations require no corrective action and result in no penalty.)

For example, the OSHA point-of-operation guarding provisions, contained in paragraph 1910.212(a)(3), require the guarding device to…*be in conformance with any appropriate standards thereof, or in the absence of applicable specific standards, shall be so designed and constructed as to prevent the operator from having any part of his body in the danger zone during the operating cycle.* The terms applicable standards or appropriate standards, as used in the context of 29 CFR 1910.212, are references to those private consensus standards that were adopted (source standards) or incorporated by reference in the OSHA standards.

In some instances, a specific national consensus standard (that is not incorporated by reference or a source standard), such as an ANSI standard for a particular machine, may be used for guidance purposes to assist employers in preventing an operator from having any body part in the machine danger zone during the operating cycle. Also, OSHA may, in appropriate cases, use these consensus standards as evidence that machine hazards are recognized and that there are feasible means of correcting the hazard. On the other hand, some national consensus standards may sanction practices that provide less employee protection than that provided by compliance with the relevant OSHA provisions. In these cases, compliance with the specific consensus standard provision would not constitute compliance with the relevant OSHA requirement.

# Recognizing Amputation Hazards

To prevent employee amputations, you and your employees must first be able to recognize the contributing factors, such as the hazardous energy associated with your machinery and the specific employee activities performed with the mechanical operation. Understanding the mechanical components of machinery, the hazardous mechanical motion that occurs at or near these components and specific employee activities performed in conjunction with machinery operation will help employees avoid injury.

## Hazardous Mechanical Components

Three types of mechanical components present amputation hazards:

**Point of Operation** is the area of the machine where the machine performs work – i.e., mechanical actions that occur at the point of operation, such as cutting, shaping, boring, and forming.

**Power-Transmission Apparatus** is all components of the mechanical system that transmit energy, such as flywheels, pulleys, belts, chains, couplings, connecting rods, spindles, cams, and gears.

**Other Moving Parts** are the parts of the machine that move while the machine is operating, such as reciprocating, rotating, and transverse moving parts as well as lead mechanisms and auxiliary parts of the machine.

## Hazardous Mechanical Motions

A wide variety of mechanical motion is potentially hazardous.  Here are the basic types of hazardous mechanical motions:

**Rotating Motion** (*Figure 1*) is circular motion such as action generated by rotating collars, couplings, cams, clutches, flywheels, shaft ends, and spindles that may grip clothing or otherwise force a body part into a dangerous location. Even smooth surfaced rotating machine parts can be hazardous. Projections such as screws or burrs on the rotating part increase the hazard potential.

*Figure 1* Rotating Motion

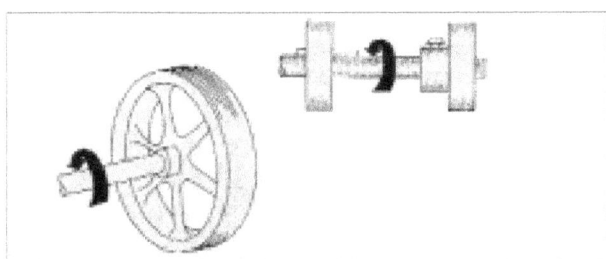

**Reciprocating Motion** (*Figure 2*) is back-and-forth or up-and-down motion that may strike or entrap an employee between a moving part and a fixed object.

*Figure 2* Reciprocating Motion

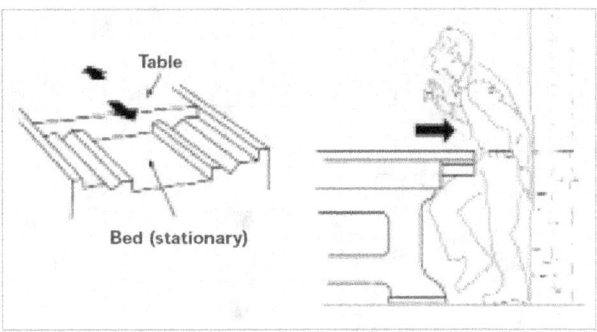

**Transversing Motion** (*Figure 3*) is motion in a straight, continuous line that may strike or catch an employee in a pinch or shear point created by the moving part and a fixed object.

*Figure 3* Transversing Motion

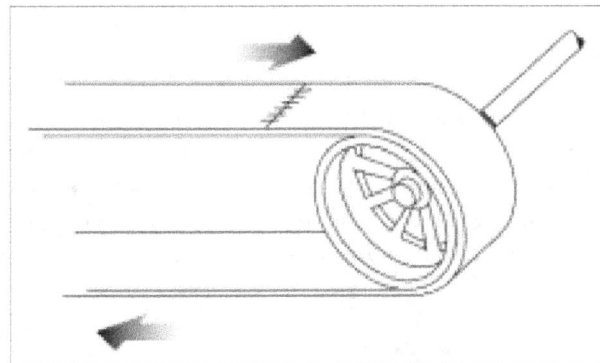

**Cutting Action** (*Figure 4*) is the action that cuts material and the associated machine motion may be rotating, reciprocating, or transverse.

*Figure 4* Cutting Action

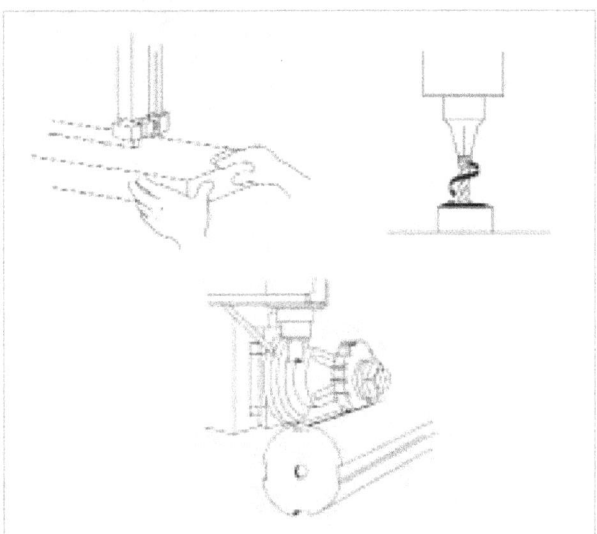

**Punching Action** (*Figure 5*) begins when power causes the machine to hit a slide (ram) to stamp or blank metal or other material. The hazard occurs at the point of operation where the employee typically inserts, holds, or withdraws the stock by hand.

*Figure 5* Punching Action

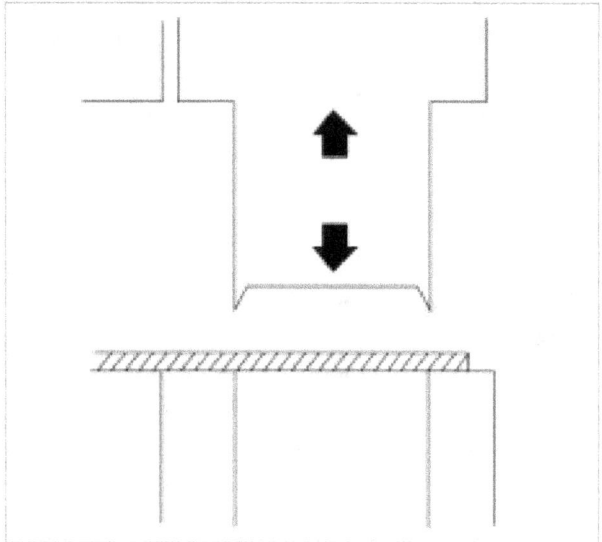

**Shearing Action** (*Figure 6*) involves applying power to a slide or knife in order to trim or shear metal or other materials. The hazard occurs at the point of operation where the employee typically inserts, holds, or withdraws the stock by hand.

*Figure 6* Shearing Action

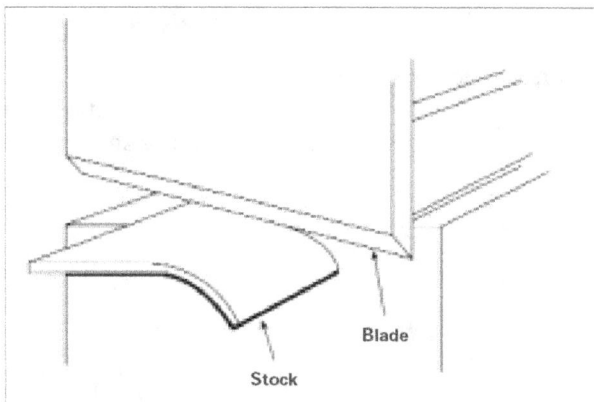

**Bending Action** (*Figure 7*) is power applied to a slide to draw or stamp metal or other materials in a bending motion. The hazard occurs at the point of operation where the employee typically inserts, holds, or withdraws the stock by hand.

*Figure 7* Bending Action

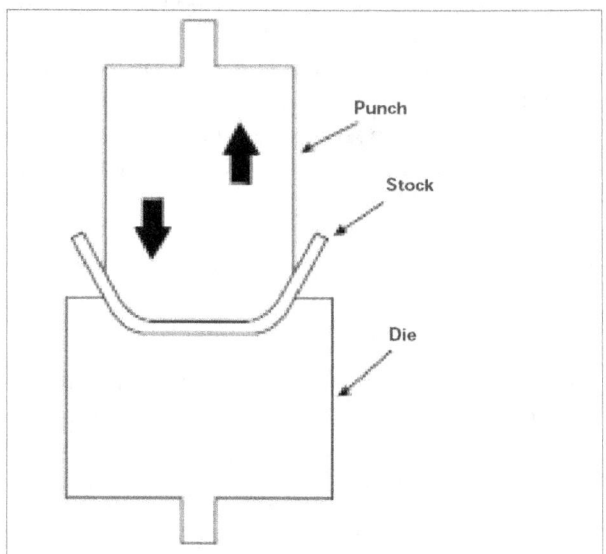

**In-Running Nip Points** (*Figure 8*), also known as "pinch points," develop when two parts move together and at least one moves in rotary or circular motion. In-running nip points occur whenever machine parts move toward each other or when one part moves past a stationary object. Typical nip points include gears, rollers, belt drives, and pulleys.

*Figure 8* In-Running Nip Points

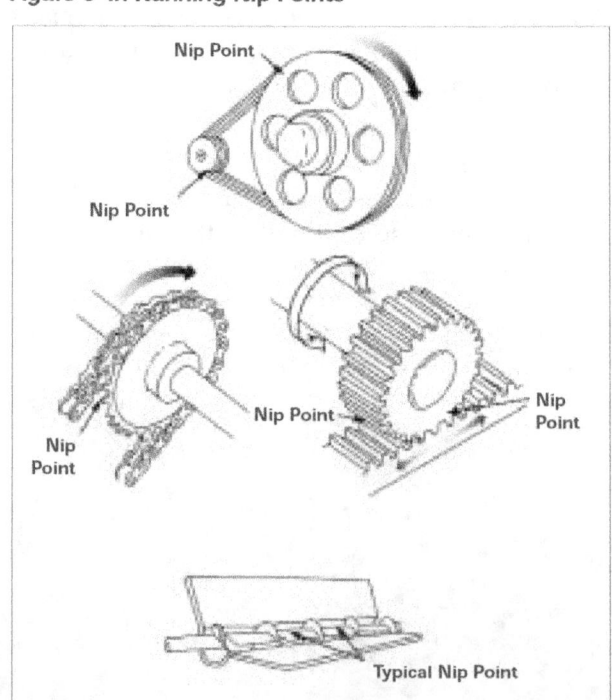

## Hazardous Activities

Employees operating and caring for machinery perform various activities that present potential amputation hazards.

Machine set-up/threading/preparation,*
Machine inspection,*
Normal production operations,
Clearing jams,*
Machine adjustments,*
Cleaning of machine,*
Lubricating of machine parts,* and
Scheduled and unscheduled maintenance.*

* These activities are servicing and/or maintenance activities.

## Hazard Analysis

You can help prevent workplace amputations by looking at your workplace operations and identifying the hazards associated with the use and care of the machine. A hazard analysis is a technique that focuses on the relationship between the employee, the task, the tools, and the environment. When evaluating work activities for potential amputation hazards, you need to consider the entire machine operation production process, the machine modes of operation, individual activities associated with the operation, servicing and maintenance of the machine, and the potential for injury to employees.

The results from the analysis may then be used as a basis to design machine safeguarding and an overall energy control (lockout/tagout) program. This is likely to result in fewer employee amputations; safer, more effective work methods; reduced workers' compensation costs; and increased employee productivity and morale.

# Controlling Amputation Hazards

Safeguarding is essential for protecting employees from needless and preventable injury. A good rule to remember is:

*Any machine part, function, or process that may cause injury must be safeguarded.*

In this booklet, the term *primary safeguarding methods* refers to machine guarding techniques that are intended to prevent or greatly reduce the chance that an employee will have an amputation injury. Refer to the OSHA general industry (e.g., Subpart O) and construction (e.g., Subparts I and N) standards for specific guarding requirements. Many of these standards address preventive methods (such as using barrier guards or two-hand tripping devices) as primary control measures; while other OSHA standards allow guarding techniques (such as a self-adjustable table saw guard) that reduce the likelihood of injury. Other less protective safeguarding methods (such as safe work methods) that do not satisfactorily protect employees from the machine hazard areas are considered secondary control methods.

Machine safeguarding must be supplemented by an effective energy control (lockout/tagout) program that ensures that employees are protected from hazardous energy sources during machine servicing and maintenance work activities. Lockout/tagout plays an essential role in the prevention and control of workplace amputations. In terms of controlling amputation hazards, employees are protected from hazardous machine work activities either by: 1) effective machine safeguarding, or 2) lockout/tagout where safeguards are rendered ineffective or do not protect employees from hazardous energy during servicing and maintenance operations.

Additionally, there are some servicing activities, such as lubricating, cleaning, releasing jams and making machine adjustments that are minor in nature and are performed during normal production operations. It is not necessary to lockout/tagout a machine if the activity is routine, repetitive and integral to the production operation provided that you use an alternative control method that affords effective protection from the machine's hazardous energy sources.

## Safeguarding Machinery

The employer is responsible for safeguarding machines and should consider this need when purchasing machinery. Almost all new machinery is available with safeguards installed by the manufacturer, but used equipment may not be.

If machinery has no safeguards, you may be able to purchase safeguards from the original machine manufacturer or from an after-market manufacturer. You can also build and install the safeguards in-house. Safeguarding equipment should be designed and installed only by technically qualified professionals. If possible, the original equipment manufacturer should review the safeguard design to ensure that it will protect employees without interfering with the operation of the machine or creating additional hazards.

Regardless of the source of safeguards, the guards and devices used need to be compatible with a machine's operation and designed to ensure safe operator use. The type of operation, size, and shape of stock, method of feeding, physical layout of the work area, and production requirements all affect the selection of safeguards. Also, safeguards should be designed with the machine operator in mind as a guarding method that interferes with the operation of the machine may cause employees to override them. To ensure effective and safe operator use, guards and devices should suit the operation.

The Performance Criteria for Safeguarding [ANSI B11.19-2003] national consensus standard provides valuable guidance as the standard addresses the design, construction, installation, operation and maintenance of the safeguarding used to protect employees from machine hazards. The following safeguarding method descriptions are, in part, structured like and, in many ways are similar to this national consensus standard.

---

The *Performance Criteria for Safeguarding* [ANSI B11.19-2003] defines safeguarding as the *protection of personnel from hazards by the use of guards, safeguarding devices awareness devices, safeguarding methods, or safe work procedures.* The following ANSI B11.19 definitions describe the various types of safeguarding:

**Guard:** A barrier that prevents exposure to an identified hazard.

**Safeguarding device:** A device that detects or prevents inadvertent access to a hazard.

NOTE: The 1990 ANSI B11.19 term *Safeguarding device* was modified to *Safeguarding (Protective) Device* in the revised 2003 ANSI standard and the new term includes a detection component. Devices that detect, but do not prevent employee

---

exposure to machine hazards are not considered by OSHA to be primary safeguarding methods.

**Awareness device:** A barrier, signal or sign that warns individuals of an impending, approaching or present hazard.

**Safeguarding method:** Safeguarding implemented to protect individuals from hazards by the physical arrangement of distance, holding, openings, or positioning of the machine or machine production system to ensure that the operator cannot reach the hazard.

**Safe work procedures:** Formal written instructions developed by the user which describe how a task is to be performed.

## Primary Safeguarding Methods

Two primary methods are used to safeguard machines: guards and some types of safeguarding devices. Guards provide physical barriers that prevent access to danger areas. Safeguarding devices either prevent or detect operator contact with the point of operation or stop potentially hazardous machine motion if any part of an individual's body is within the hazardous portion of the machine. Both types of safeguards need to be properly designed, constructed, installed, used and maintained in good operating condition to ensure employee protection.

---

**Criteria for Machine Safeguarding**

- Prevents employee contact with the hazard area during machine operation.
- Avoids creating additional hazards.
- Is secure, tamper-resistant, and durable.
- Avoids interfering with normal operation of the machine.
- Allows for safe lubrication and maintenance.

---

## Guards

Guards usually are preferable to other control methods because they are physical barriers that enclose dangerous machine parts and prevent employee contact with them. To be effective, guards must be strong and fastened by any secure method that prevents the guard from being inadvertently dislodged or removed. Guards typically are designed with screws, bolts and lock fasteners and usually a tool is necessary to unfasten and remove them. Generally, guards are designed not to obstruct the operator's view or to prevent employees from doing a job.

In some cases, guarding may be used as an alternative to lockout/tagout because employees can safely service or maintain machines with a guard in place. For example, polycarbonate and wire-mesh guards provide greater visibility and can be used to allow maintenance employees to safely observe system components. In other instances, employees may safely access machine areas, without locking or tagging out, to perform maintenance work (such as machine cleaning or oiling tasks) because the hazardous machine components remain effectively guarded.

Guards must not create additional hazards such as pinch points or shear points between guards and other machine parts. Guard openings should be small enough to prevent employees from accessing danger areas. (See *Table 1* and *Figures 9 through 12* for commonly used machine guards.)

*Figure 9* **Fixed Guard on a Power Press**

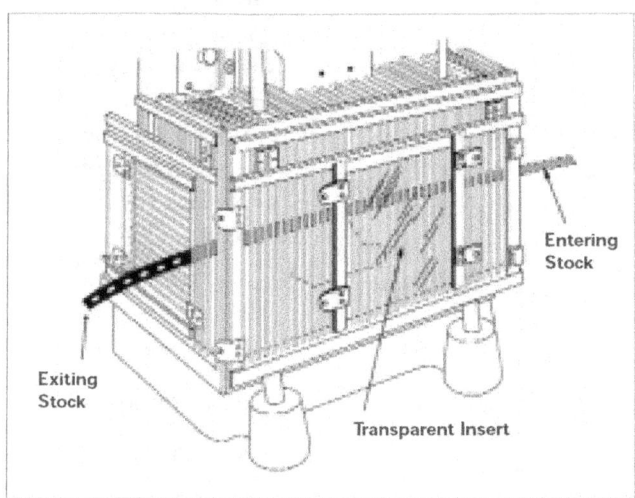

*Figure 10* **Power Press with an Adjustable Barrier Guard**

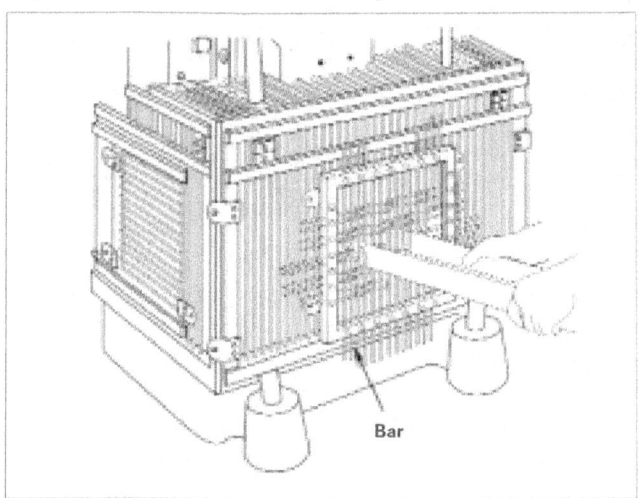

*Figure 11* **Self-Adjusting Guard on a Radial Saw**

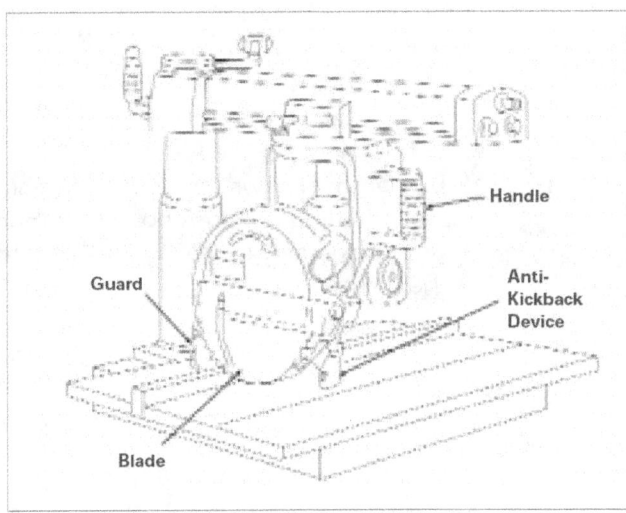

*Figure 12* **Interlocked Guard on a Roll Make-up Machine**

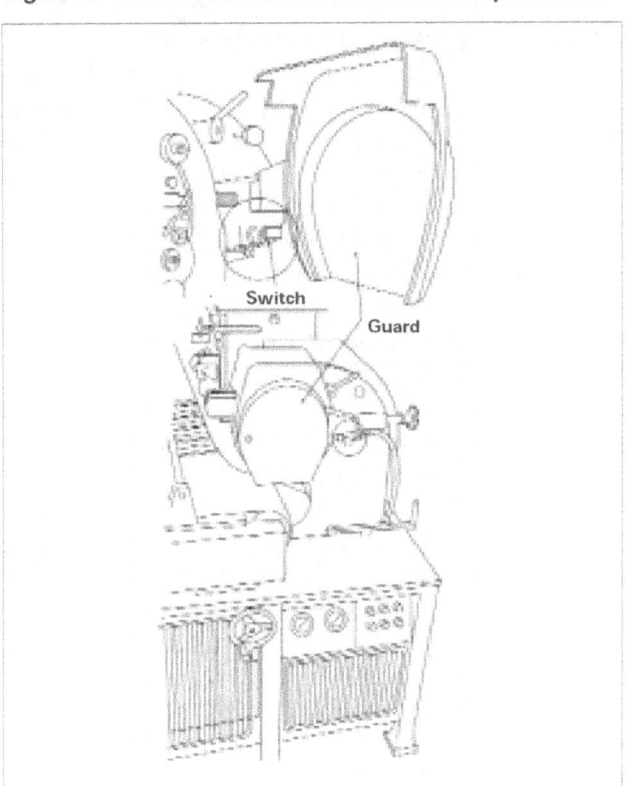

*Table 1.* Commonly Used Machine Guards

| Types of Machine Guards | | | |
|---|---|---|---|
| **Type** | **Method of Safeguarding** | **Advantages** | **Limitations** |
| Fixed | Barrier that allows for stock feeding but does not permit operator to reach the danger area. | • Can be constructed to suit many applications.<br>• Permanently encloses the point of operation or hazard area.<br>• Provides protection against machine repeat.<br>• Allows simple, in-plant construction, with minimal maintenance. | • Sometimes not practical for changing production runs involving different size stock or feeding methods.<br>• Machine adjustment and repair often require guard removal.<br>• Other means of protecting maintenance personnel often required (lockout/tagout). |
| Adjustable | Barrier that adjusts for a variety of production operations. | • Can be constructed to suit many applications.<br>• Can be adjusted to admit varying stock sizes. | • May require frequent maintenance or adjustment.<br>• Operator may make guard ineffective. |
| Self-Adjusting | Barrier that moves according to the size of the stock entering point of operation. Guard is in place when machine is at rest and pushes away when stock enters the point of operation. | • Off-the-shelf guards are often commercially available. | • Does not provide maximum protection.<br>• May require frequent maintenance and adjustment. |
| Interlocking Barrier Guards | Shuts off or disengages power and prevents machine start-up when guard is open. Should allow for inching of machine. | • Allows access for some minor servicing work, in accordance with the lockout/tagout exception, without time-consuming removal of fixed guards. | • May require periodic maintenance or adjustment.<br>• Movable sections cannot be used for manual feeding.<br>• Some designs may be easy to defeat.<br>• Interlock control circuitry may not be used for all maintenance and servicing work. |

## Safeguarding Devices

Safeguarding devices are controls or attachments that, when properly designed, applied and used, usually prevent inadvertent access by employees to hazardous machine areas by:

• Preventing hazardous machine component operation if your hand or body part is inadvertently placed in the danger area;
• Restraining or withdrawing your hands from the danger area during machine operation;
• Requiring the use of both of your hands on machine controls (or the use of one hand if the control is mounted at a safe distance from the danger area) that are mounted at a predetermined safety distance; or
• Providing a barrier which is synchronized with the operating cycle in order to prevent entry to the danger area during the hazardous part of the cycle.

These types of engineering controls, which either prevent the start of or stop hazardous motion, may be used in place of guards or as supplemental control measures when guards alone do not adequately enclose the hazard. In order for these safeguarding devices to accomplish this requirement, they must be properly designed and installed at a predetermined safe distance from the machine's danger area. Other safeguarding devices (probe detection and safety edge devices) that merely detect, instead of prevent, inadvertent

access to a hazard are not considered primary safeguards. (See *Table 2* and *Figures 13 through 17* for the types of safeguarding devices.)

*Figure 13* **Pullback Device on a Power Press**

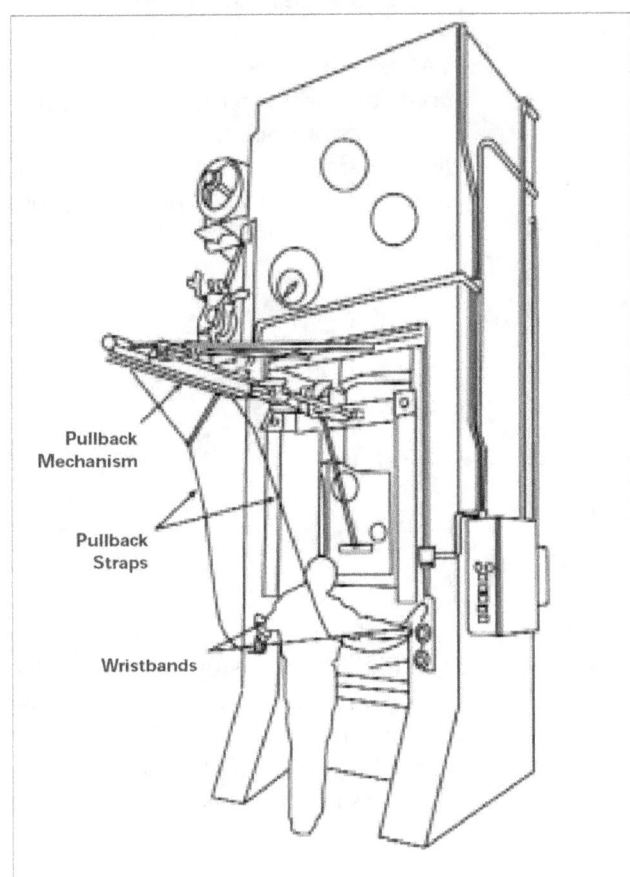

Pullback Mechanism

Pullback Straps

Wristbands

*Table 2.* **Types of Safeguarding Devices**

| Types of Machine Guards | | | |
|---|---|---|---|
| **Type** | **Method of Safeguarding** | **Advantages** | **Limitations** |
| Pullback Devices | Cords connected to operator's wrists and linked mechanically to the machine automatically withdraw the hands from the point of operation during the machine cycle. | • Allows the hands to enter the point of operation for feeding and removal.<br>• Provides protection even in the event of mechanical repeat. | • Close supervision ensures proper use and adjustment. Must be inspected prior to each operator change or machine set-up.<br>• Limits operator's movement and may obstruct their work space.<br>• Operator may easily make device ineffective by not adjusting the device properly. |

*Table 2.* Types of Safeguarding Devices (continued)

| Types of Machine Guards | | | |
|---|---|---|---|
| **Type** | **Method of Safeguarding** | **Advantages** | **Limitations** |
| Restraint Devices | Wrists are connected by cords and secured to a fixed anchor point which limit operator's hands from reaching the point of oper-ation at any time. | • Simple, few moving parts; requires little maintenance.<br>• Operator cannot reach into the danger area.<br>• Little risk of mechanical failure; provides protec-tion even in the event of mechanical repeat. | • Close supervision re-quired to ensure proper use and adjustment. Must be inspected prior to each operator change or machine set-up.<br>• Operator must use hand tools to enter the point of operation.<br>• Limits the movement of the operator; may obstruct work space around operator.<br>• Operator may easily make device ineffective by dis-connecting the device. |
| Presence-Sensing Devices | Interlock into the machine's control system to stop operation when the sens-ing field (photoelectric, radio frequency, or electro-magnetic) is disturbed. | • Adjusts to fit different stock sizes.<br>• Allows access to load and unload the machine.<br>• Allows access to the guarded area for main-tenance and set-up activities. | • Restricted to machines that stop operating cycle before operator can reach into danger area (e.g., machines with partial revolution clutches or hydraulic machines).<br>• Must be carefully main-tained and adjusted.<br>• Does not protect operator in the event of a mechanical failure.<br>• Operator may make device ineffective. |
| Presence-Sensing Mats | Interlock into machine's control system to stop operation when a predeter-mined weight is applied to the mat. A manual reset switch must be located out-side the protected zone. | • Full visibility and access to the work area.<br>• Install as a perimeter guard or over an entire area.<br>• Configure for many applications. | • Restricted to machines that stop operating cycle before operator can reach into danger area (e.g., machines with part-revolution clutches or hydraulic machines).<br>• Some chemicals can degrade the mats.<br>• Does not protect operator during mechanical failures. |

*Table 2.* Types of Safeguarding Devices (continued)

| Types of Machine Guards | | | |
|---|---|---|---|
| **Type** | **Method of Safeguarding** | **Advantages** | **Limitations** |
| Two-Hand Control | Requires concurrent and continued use of both hands, preventing them from entering the danger area. | • Operator's hands are at a predetermined safety distance.<br>• Operator's hands are free to pick up new parts after completion of first part of cycle. | • Requires a partial cycle machine with a brake and anti-repeat feature.<br>• Operator may make devices without anti-tiedown ineffective.<br>• Protects the operator only. |
| Two-Hand Trip | Requires concurrent use of both hands, prevents them from being in danger area when machine cycle starts. | • Operator's hands are at a predetermined safety distance.<br>• Can be adapted to multiple operations.<br>• No obstruction to hand feeding. | • Operator may make devices without anti-tiedown ineffective.<br>• Protects the operator only.<br>• Sometimes impractical because distance requirements may reduce production below acceptable level.<br>• May require adjustment with tooling changes.<br>• Requires anti-repeat feature. |
| Type "A" Gate (move-able barrier) | Applicable to mechanical power presses. Provides barrier between danger area and operator (or other employees) until completion of machine cycle. | • Prevents operator from reaching into danger area during machine cycle.<br>• Provides protection from machine repeat. | • May require frequent inspection and regular maintenance.<br>• May interfere with operator's ability to see work. |
| Type "B" Gate (move-able barrier) | Applicable to mechanical power presses and press brakes. Provides a barrier between danger area and operator (or other employees) during the down-stroke. | • May increase production by allowing the operator to remove and feed the press on the upstroke. | • Can only be used on machines with a part-revolution clutch or hydraulic machines.<br>• May require frequent inspection and regular maintenance.<br>• May interfere with the operator's ability to see work. |

*Figure 14* Restraint Device on a Power Press

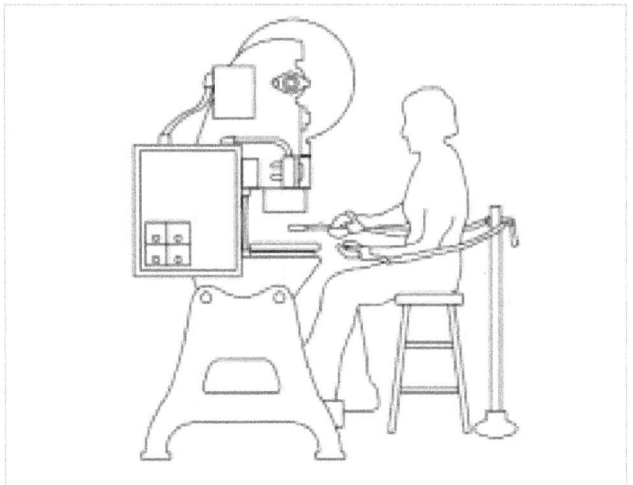

*Figure 15* Presence-Sensing Device on a Power Press

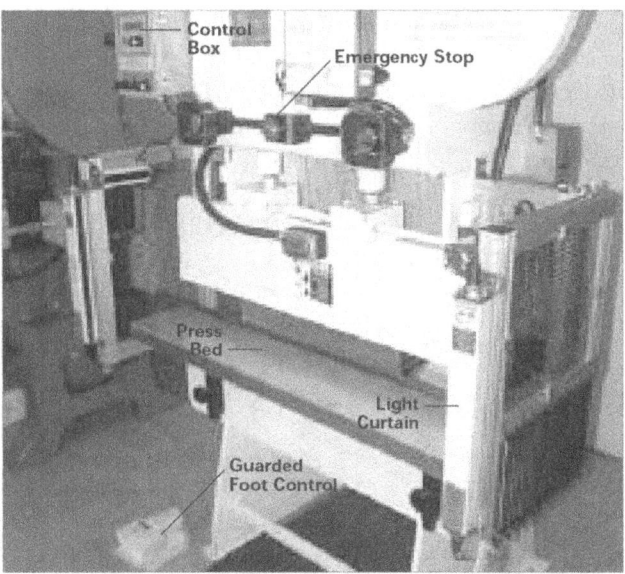

*Figure 16* Two-Hand Control

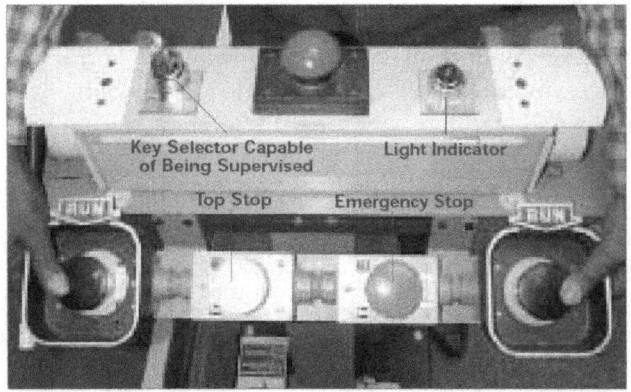

*Figure 17* Power Press with a Gate

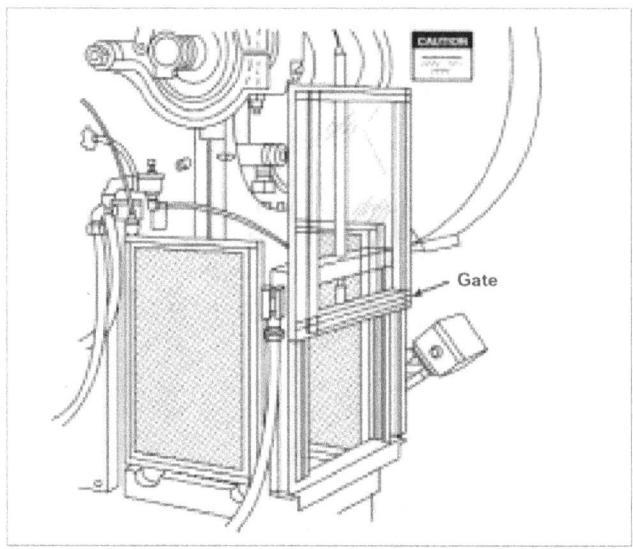

## Secondary Safeguarding Methods

Other safeguarding methods, such as those described in the *Performance Criteria for Safeguarding* (ANSI B11.19-2003), may also provide employees with some protection from machine hazards. Detection safeguarding devices, awareness devices, safeguarding methods and safe work procedures are described in this section. These methods provide a lesser degree of employee protection than the primary safeguarding methods and they are considered secondary control measures as they do not prevent employees from placing or having any part of their bodies in the hazardous machine areas.

Secondary safeguarding methods are acceptable only when guards or safeguarding devices (that prevent you from being exposed to machine hazards) cannot be installed due to reasons of infeasibility. Where it is feasible to use primary safeguarding methods, secondary safeguarding methods may supplement these primary control measures; however, these secondary safeguarding methods must not be used in place of primary safeguarding methods.

## Probe Detection and Safety Edge Devices

A probe detection device (sometimes referred to as a *ring guard*) detects the presence or absence of a person's hand or finger by encircling all or part of the machine hazard area. The *ring guard* makes you aware of your hand's entry into a hazardous area and usually stops or prevents a hazardous machine cycle or stroke, thereby reducing the likelihood of injuring yourself in the point of operation. These types of detection devices are commonly used on spot welders, riveters, staplers and stackers because primary safeguarding methods are not possible. However, probe detection devices do not prevent inadvertent access to the point-of-operation danger area; rather, they serve as a warning mechanism and may prevent the initiation of or stop the machine cycle if an employee's hand or finger(s) is too close to the hazard area.

A safety edge device (sometimes called a *bump switch*) is another type of safeguard that detects the presence of an employee when they are in contact with the device's sensing edge. A safety edge device protects employees by initiating a stop command when the sensing surface detects the presence of a person; however, they do not usually, when used by themselves, prevent inadvertent access to machine danger areas. Therefore, additional guarding or safeguarding devices must be provided to prevent employee exposure to a machine hazard.

## Awareness Devices

Awareness devices warn employees of an impending, approaching or present hazard. The first type is an awareness barrier which allows access to machine danger areas, but it is designed to contact the employee, creating an awareness that he or she is close to the danger point. Awareness signals, through the use of recognizable audible or visual signals, are other devices that alert employees to an approaching or present hazard. Lastly, awareness signs are used to notify employees of the nature of the hazard and to provide instructions and training information. OSHA standard 1910.145 provides design, application, and use specifications for accident prevention (danger, caution, safety instruction) signs and (danger, caution, warning) tags.

## Safeguarding Methods

Safeguarding methods protect employees from hazards by the physical arrangement of distance, holding, openings or the positioning of the machine components to ensure that the operator cannot reach the hazard. Some safeguarding work methods include safe distance safeguarding, safe holding safeguarding and safe opening safeguarding. Requirements for these secondary control measures may be found in ANSI B11.19-2003. Proper training and supervision are essential to ensure that these secondary safeguarding methods are being used properly. Safeguarding work methods may require the use of awareness devices, including the use of accident prevention signs where there is a need for warning or safety instruction.

## Safe Distance Safeguarding

Safeguarding by safe distance (by location) may involve an operator holding and supporting a work-piece with both hands at a predetermined minimum safe distance or, if both hands cannot be used to hold the work-piece at a distance so that the operator cannot reach the hazard with the free hand. For example, the feeding process itself can create a distance safeguard if the operators maintain a safe distance between their hands and the point of operation. Additionally, where material position gauges are used, they need to be of sufficient height and size to prevent slipping of the material past the gauges.

Another example of a safe distance safeguarding method is the use of gravity feed methods that reduce or eliminate employee exposure to machine hazards as the part slides down a chute into the point of operation. Automatic and semiautomatic feeding and ejection methods can also protect the employee by minimizing or eliminating employee exposure with potentially hazardous machinery components. An employee places the part in a magazine which is then fed into the point of operation. Automatic and semiautomatic ejection methods include pneumatic (jet of air), magnetic, mechanical (such as an arm), or vacuum. *Figures 18 and 19* illustrate different types of automatic feeding and ejecting methods.

*Figure 18* **Power Press with a Plunger Feed**

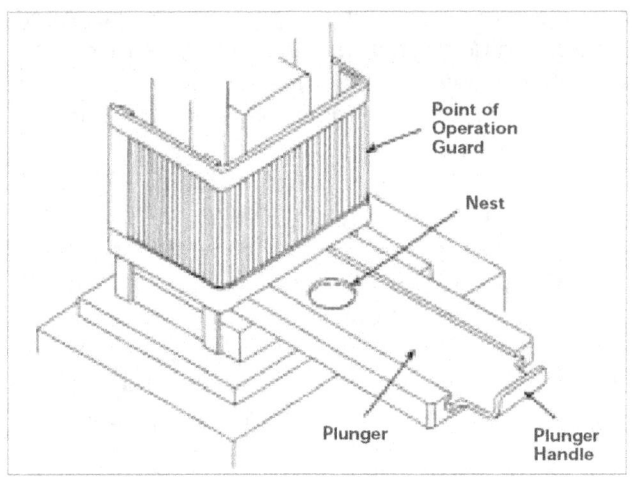

Figure 19 Shuttle Ejection Mechanism

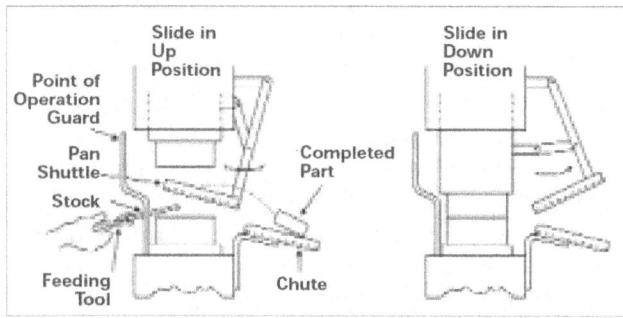

## Safe Holding Safeguarding (Safe Work-Piece Safeguarding)

Operator's hands are maintained away from the hazardous portion of the machine cycle by requiring that both hands are used to hold or support the work-piece, or by requiring that one hand holds the work-piece while the other hand operates the machine. For instance, if the stock is several feet long and only one end of the stock is being worked on, the operator may be able to hold the opposite end while performing the work. The operator's body parts are out of the machine hazard area during the hazardous portion of the machine cycle. However, this work method only protects the operator.

## Safe Opening Safeguarding

This method limits access to the machine hazardous areas by the size of the opening or by closing off the danger zone access when the work-piece is in place in the machine. Operators are prevented from reaching the hazard area during the machine operation; however, employee access to the danger area is not adequately guarded when the work-piece is not in place.

## Safe Work Procedures

Safe work procedures are formal, written instructions which describe how a task is to be performed. These procedures should incorporate appropriate safe work practices, such as prohibiting employees from wearing loose clothing or jewelry and requiring the securing of long hair with nets or caps. Clothing, jewelry, long hair, and even gloves can get entangled in moving machine parts.

## Complementary Equipment

Complementary equipment is used in conjunction with selected safeguarding techniques and it is, by itself, not a safeguarding method. Some common complementary equipment used to augment machine safeguarding include:

## Emergency Stop Devices

Emergency stop devices are designed to be used in reaction to an incident or hazardous situation and, as such, are not considered machine safeguarding. These devices, such as buttons, rope-pulls, cable-pulls, or pressure-sensitive body bars, neither detect nor prevent employee exposure to machine hazards; rather they initiate an action to stop hazardous motion when an employee recognizes a hazard and activates them. (See Figure 20.)

Figure 20 Safety Tripod on a Rubber Mill

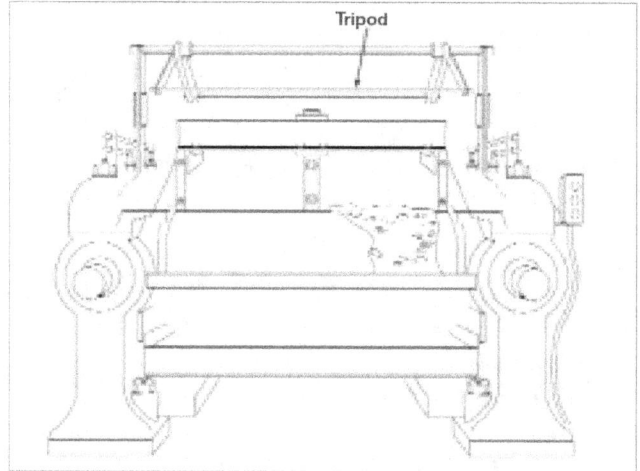

## Work-Holding Equipment

Work-holding equipment is not used to feed or remove the work-piece, but rather to hold it in place during the hazardous portion of the machine cycle. Clamps, jigs, fixtures and back gauges are examples of work-holding equipment. This equipment may be used to reduce or eliminate the need for an employee to place their hands in the hazard area.

## Feeding and Ejection Systems

A feeding and ejection system (e.g., a gravity fed chute; semi-automatic and automatic feeding and ejection equipment), by itself, does not constitute secondary safeguarding. However, the use of properly designed feed and ejection mechanisms can protect employees by minimizing or eliminating the need for them to be in a hazard area during the hazardous motion of the machine.

## Hand-Feeding Tools

Operators can use tools to feed and remove material into and from machines so as to keep their hands away from the point of operation. However, this must be done only in conjunction with the guards and safeguarding devices described previously. Hand tools are not point-of-operation guarding or safeguarding devices and they need to be designed to allow employees' hands to remain outside of the machine danger area. Using hand tools requires close supervision to ensure that the operator does not bypass their use to increase production. It is recommended that these tools be stored near the operation to promote their use.

To prevent injury and repetitive trauma disorders, hand-feeding tools should be shatterproof and ergonomically designed for the specific task being performed. (*Figure 21* shows typical hand-feeding tools.)

*Figure 21* Typical Hand-Feeding Tools

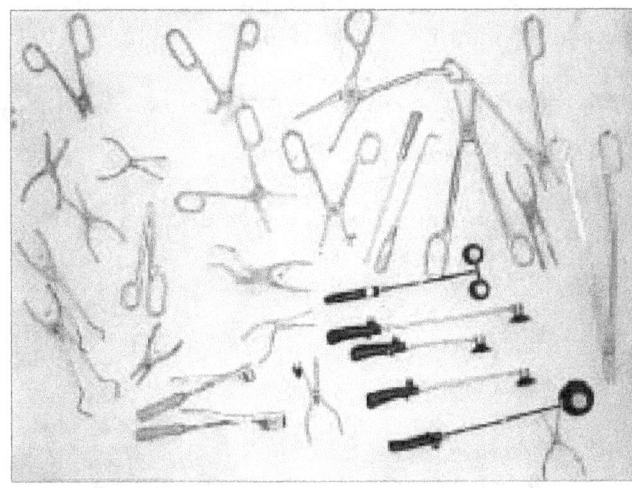

### Foot Controls

Foot controls that are not securely fixed at a safe distance do not constitute machine safeguarding because they do not keep the operator's hands out of the danger area. If you use foot-actuated controls that are not single-control safeguarding devices, they will need to be used with some type of guard or other safeguarding device.

Improperly used foot-actuated controls may increase productivity, but the freedom of hand movement increases the risk of a point-of-operation injury or amputation. Foot controls must be guarded to prevent accidental activation by another employee or by falling material. Do not ride the foot pedal. Ensure that the machine control circuit is properly designed to prevent continuous cycling. (See *Figure 22* for an example of a properly guarded foot control.)

*Figure 22*
**Properly Guarded Foot Control**

### Administrative Issues

As an employer, you need to consider housekeeping practices, employee apparel, and employee training. Implement good housekeeping practices to promote safe working conditions around machinery by doing the following:

*   Remove slip, trip, and fall hazards from the areas surrounding machines;
*   Use drip pans when oiling equipment;
*   Remove waste stock as it is generated;
*   Make the work area large enough for machine operation and maintenance; and
*   Place machines away from high traffic areas to reduce employee distraction.

Employees should not wear loose-fitting clothing, jewelry, or other items that could become entangled in machinery, and long hair should be worn under a cap or otherwise contained to prevent entanglement in moving machinery.

Adequate instruction in the safe use and care of machines and supervised on-the-job training are essential in preventing amputation injuries. Only trained employees should operate machinery.

---

**Train Employees in the Following:**

*   All hazards in the work area, including machine-specific hazards;
*   Machine operating procedures, lockout/tagout procedures and safe work practices;
*   The purpose and proper use of machine safeguards; and
*   All procedures for responding to safeguarding problems such as immediately reporting unsafe conditions such as missing or damaged guards and violations of safe operating practices to supervisors.

---

In addition to employee instruction and training, employers need to provide adequate supervision to reinforce safe practices. Take disciplinary action to enforce safe work practices and working conditions.

### Inspection and Maintenance

Good inspection, maintenance and repair procedures contribute significantly to the safety of the maintenance crew as well as to the operators. To ensure the integrity of the machinery and machine safeguards, a proactive, versus a *break-down* maintenance program needs to be established based upon the:

- Manufacturer's recommendations;
- Good engineering practice; and
- Any applicable OSHA provisions (such as the mechanical power press inspection and maintenance requirements, contained in 1910.217(e)).

### Lockout/Tagout

OSHA's lockout/tagout (LOTO) standard, 29 CFR 1910.147, establishes minimum performance requirements for controlling hazardous energy and it is intended to complement and augment machine safeguarding practices. The lockout/tagout standard applies only if employees are exposed to hazardous energy during servicing/maintenance activities. An employer may avoid the requirements of the LOTO standard if the safeguarding method eliminates your employees' exposure to the machine danger area during the servicing or maintenance work by using Machinery and Machine Guarding methods in accordance with the requirements contained in 29 CFR 1910, Subpart O.

Additionally, because some minor servicing may have to be performed during normal production operations, an employer may be exempt from LOTO in some instances. Minor tool changes and adjustments and other minor servicing operations, which take place during normal production operations, are not covered by lockout/tagout if they are routine, repetitive and integral to the use of the machine for production and if work is performed using alternative effective protective measures that provide effective employee protection.

In short, a hazardous energy control program is a critical part of an overall strategy to prevent workplace amputations during machine servicing and maintenance activities, such as during the setting up of machines for production purposes, bypassing guards to clear jams or lubricate parts, and inspecting, adjusting, replacing, or otherwise servicing machine parts. Machine amputations occur when an employer does not have or fails to implement practices and procedures to disable and control a machine's energy sources during machine servicing and maintenance work.

# Specific Machine Hazards and Safeguarding Methods

As discussed earlier, 8,450 known non-fatal amputation cases (involving days away from work) occurred in 2005 for all of private industry. The most prevalent injury source was, by far, machinery, which accounted for approximately 60% (5,080 instances) of the amputation cases.[1] The machinery listed here cause amputation injuries, and appropriate safeguarding and hazardous energy control (lockout/tagout) methods are addressed in this section. Employers need to consult the OSHA standard for specific machinery to ensure compliance with all requirements. For other types of hazardous sources of injury, see Appendix B.

| Machinery Associated with Amputations |
|---|
| 1. Mechanical Power Presses |
| 2. Power Press Brakes |
| 3. Powered and Non-Powered Conveyors |
| 4. Printing Presses |
| 5. Roll-Forming and Roll-Bending Machines |
| 6. Shearing Machines |
| 7. Food Slicers |
| 8. Meat Grinders |
| 9. Meat-Cutting Band Saws |
| 10. Drill Presses |
| 11. Milling Machines |
| 12. Grinding Machines |
| 13. Slitters |

### Hazards of Mechanical Power Presses

Although there are three major types of power presses—mechanical, hydraulic, and pneumatic—the machinery that accounts for a large number of workplace amputations are mechanical power presses.

In mechanical power presses, tools or dies are mounted on a slide, or ram, which operates in a controlled, reciprocating motion toward and away from the stationary bed or anvil containing the lower die. When the upper and lower dies press together – to punch, shear or form – the work-piece, the desired piece is produced. Once the downstroke is completed, the re-formed work-piece

[1] U.S. Department of Labor, Bureau of Labor Statistics (BLS); Annual Survey data, Table R25. Number of non-fatal occupational injuries or illnesses involving days away from work by source of injury or illness and selected natures of injury or illness, 2005.

is removed either automatically or manually, a new work-piece is fed into the die, and the process is repeated. (See *Figure 23*.)

*Figure 23*  Part Revolution Mechanical Power Press with a Two-Hand Control

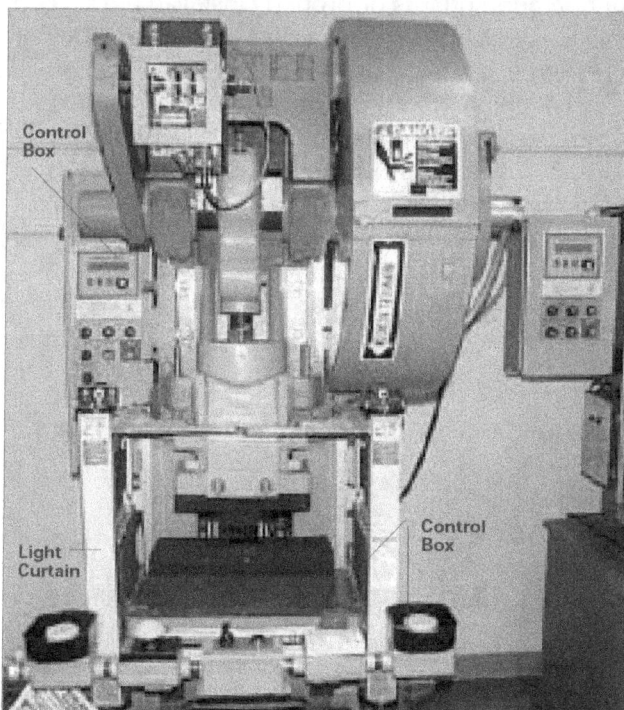

### Controls for Machines with Clutches

Certain machines can be categorized based on the type of clutch they use—full-revolution or part-revolution. Differing modes of operation for these two clutches determine the type of guarding that can be used.

Full-revolution clutches, once activated, complete a full cycle of the slide (lowering and raising of the slide) before stopping at dead center and cannot be disengaged until the cycle is complete. So, presence-sensing devices will not work and operators must be protected during the entire press operating cycle. For example, properly applied barrier guards or two-hand trip devices that are installed at a safe distance from the hazard area may be used.

Machines incorporating full-revolution clutches, such as mechanical power presses, must also incorporate a single-stroke device and anti-repeat feature.

The majority of part-revolution presses are air clutch and brake. They are designed to trap air in a chamber or tube. When the compressed air is put into these chambers, the clutch is engaged, the brake disengaged and the press

makes a single stroke. To stop the press, the reverse takes place. Thus, the part-revolution clutch can be disengaged at any time during the cycle to stop the cycle before it completes the downstroke.

For safeguarding purposes, part-revolution mechanical power presses can be equipped with presence-sensing devices, but full-revolution mechanical power presses cannot.

NOTE:  Likewise, most hydraulic power presses and their associated control systems are similar to part-revolution mechanical power presses in that the slide can be stopped at any point in the cycle. In order to ensure the integrity of the safety-related functions, safeguarding devices (such as presence-sensing devices) may only be used on hydraulic power presses that are properly designed and constructed (in accordance with good engineering practice) to accommodate the safeguarding system. Refer to OSHA's Machine Guarding eTool for additional information on hydraulic presses.

Amputations occurring from the point of operation hazards are the most common types of injuries associated with mechanical power presses. Improperly applied safeguarding methods (such as using a guard with more than maximum allowable openings or 2-hand palm buttons that are mounted within the safety distance of the press) may allow operators unsafe access to the press's hazardous area. These unsafe conditions may result in an amputation when an operator, for example, instinctively reaches into the point of operation to adjust a misaligned part or release a jam. Also, amputations occur when an operator's normal feeding rhythm is interrupted, resulting in inadvertent placement of the operator's hands in the point of operation. Such injuries usually happen while the operator is riding the foot pedal.  Additionally, some amputations are linked to mechanical (such as the failure of a single-stroke linkage), electrical (such as a control relay failure), or pneumatic (such as the loss of air pressure to the clutch/brake) machine component failure.

Examples of inadequate or ineffective safeguarding and hazardous energy control practices include the following:

- Guards and devices disabled to increase production, to allow the insertion of small-piece work, or to allow better viewing of the operation.
- Two-hand trips/controls bridged or tied-down to allow initiation of the press cycle using only one hand.
- Devices such as pullbacks or restraints improperly adjusted.

- Controls of a single-operator press bypassed by having a coworker activate the controls while the operator positions or aligns parts in the die, or repairs or troubleshoots the press.
- Failure to properly disable, isolate press energy sources, and lockout/tagout presses before an employee performs servicing or maintenance work.

---

### Case History #1
While using an unguarded, foot-pedal-operated, full-revolution mechanical power press that made trip collars for wood stoves, an employee used his hands to feed and remove finished parts and scrap metal. He placed the completed part to the left side of the press, and then turned to place the scrap in the bin behind him. As he turned back to face the press, he inadvertently stepped on the foot pedal and activated the press while his hand was in the die area. His left hand was amputated at the wrist.

### Case History #2
An employee was operating an unguarded 10-ton, full-revolution mechanical power press to stamp mailbox parts, and using a hand tool to load the press, she placed her left hand in the lower die to reposition a misaligned part. At the same time, she inadvertently depressed the foot pedal, activating the press and crushing her left index finger.

### Case History #3
A power press operator and helper were instructed to temporarily halt production and each employee decided to perform servicing tasks. The operator had a problem with a hydraulic fluid leak and decided to deflect the liquid spray by installing a temporary barrier while, at the same time, the helper decided to clean up the metal chips from the press area. The operator then activated the press and repositioned the press slide in order to install the cardboard barrier. This mechanical power press action fatally crushed the helper's head because his head was between the dies while he was in the process of cleaning up the metal chips.

Source: OSHA IMIS Accident Investigation Database.

---

## Safeguarding Mechanical Power Presses
Mechanical power presses are extremely versatile and selecting appropriate safeguarding methods depends on the specific press design and use. You should consider the press, the type of clutch used, the stock size, the length of production runs, and the method of feeding.

You can use primary safeguarding methods, such as guards or safeguarding devices, to prevent injuries. For example, 29 CFR 1910.217 requires employers to provide and ensure the use of point of operation guards or properly installed devices on every operation performed on a press when the die opening is greater than $1/4$ inch.

In addition, guards must conform to the maximum permissible openings of Table O-10 of 29 CFR 1910.217. Guards must prevent entry of hands or fingers into the point of operation through, over, under, or around the guard.

---

### Mechanical Power Press Safeguarding Methods by Clutch Type

| Full-Revolution Clutch | Part-Revolution Clutch |
| --- | --- |
| Point of Operation Guard | Point of Operation Guard |
| Pullback | Pullback |
| Restraint | Restraint |
| Type A Gate | Type A Gate |
| Two-Hand Trip | Type B Gate* |
| | Two-Hand Control* |
| | Presence-Sensing Device* |

*"Hands-in-Die" operations require additional safeguarding measures: See 1910.217(c)(5).

---

### Mechanical power press point of operation safeguards must accomplish the following goals:

- Prevent or stop the normal press stroke if the operator's hands are in the point of operation; or
- Prevent the operator from reaching into the point of operation as the die closes; or
- Withdraw the operator's hands if inadvertently placed in the point of operation as the die closes; or
- Prevent the operator from reaching the point of operation at any time; or
- Require the operator to use both hands for the machine controls that are located at such a distance that the slide completes the downward travel or stops before the operator can reach into the point of operation; or
- Enclose the point of operation before a press stroke can be started to prevent the operator from reaching into the danger area before die closure or enclose the point of operation prior to stoppage of the slide motion during the downward stroke.

Source: 29 CFR 1910.217(c)(3)(i).

### "No Hands-in-Die" Policy

In general, a "no-hands-in-die" policy needs to be implemented and followed whenever possible – that is, in the event the press is not designed for "hands-in-die" production work. Under this policy, operators must never place their hands in the die area (point-of-operation) while performing normal production operations. Adherence to this safety practice will reduce the risk of point of operation amputations.

In terms of part-revolution mechanical power presses that use a two-hand control, presence-sensing device or type B gate, OSHA does allow "hands-in-die" operation if the press control reliability and brake monitoring system requirements are met. If these press design safety features are not complied with, then employers must incorporate a "no-hands-in-die" policy.

Source: 29 CFR 1910.217(c)(5).

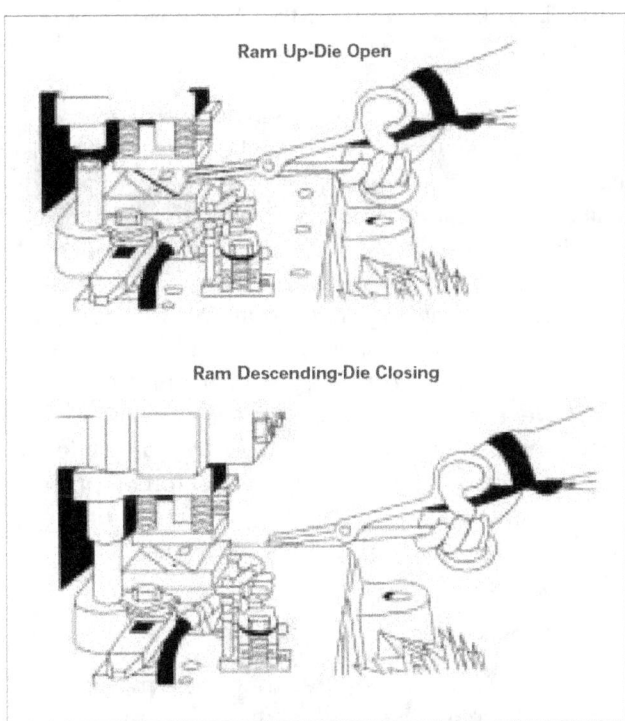

**Figure 24** Hand-Feeding Tools Used in Conjunction with Pullbacks on a Power Press

Ram Up-Die Open

Ram Descending-Die Closing

## Other Controls for Mechanical Power Press Servicing and Maintenance

Secondary safeguarding methods may be used alone or in combination (to achieve near equivalent protection) only when the employer can show that it is impossible to use any of the primary safeguarding methods. The following are some work practices, complementary equipment and energy control measures that may be used to supplement primary safeguarding:

- If employees operate presses under a "no-hands-in-die" policy using complementary feeding methods such as hand-tool feeding, employers still must protect operators through the use of primary safeguarding methods, such as a properly applied two-hand control or trip safeguarding device. Hand-tool feeding alone does not ensure that the operator's hands cannot reach the danger area. (*Figure 24* illustrates the use of hand-feeding tools in conjunction with pullbacks on a power press.)

- Removing scrap or stuck work with tools is required even when hand feeding is allowed according to 29 CFR 1910.217(d)(1)(ii). Employers must furnish and enforce the use of hand tools for freeing or removing work or scrap pieces from the die to reduce the amount of time an operator's hand is near the point of operation.
- Control point of operation hazards created when guards are removed for set-up and repair by operating the machine in the inch mode. This involves using two-hand controls (or a single control mounted at a safe distance from the machine hazards) to gradually inch the press through a stroke when the dies are being tested on part-revolution clutch presses.
- Observe energy control procedures and practices for press servicing and maintenance work. For example, the changing of dies on a mechanical power press requires the employer to establish a die-setting procedure that employs point-of-operation safeguarding method(s) such as the safe usage of an *inch* or *jog* safety device for die set-up purposes together with LOTO. These devices safely position the mechanical power press slide utilizing a point-of-operation safeguarding technique. Thus, an energy control procedure for these types of presses would

need to integrate both point-of-operation safeguarding method(s) for slide positioning as well as LOTO procedures for the die setting operation.

Additional power press energy control precautions (e.g., use of safety blocks; LOTO the press disconnect switch if re-energization presents a hazard) will be necessary if employees need to place their hands/arms in a press working area (the space between the bolster plate and the ram/slide) to perform the servicing and/or maintenance activity (such as adjusting, cleaning or repairing dies) because the *inch* or *jog* safety device will not protect employees from ram movement due to potential mechanical energy (resulting from the ram/slide position and associated gravitational force), press component or control system malfunction, or press activation by others.

---

### Minor Servicing

At times, OSHA recognizes that some minor servicing may have to be performed during normal production operations, so a lockout/tagout exception is allowed. See the 29 CFR 1910.147(a)(2)(ii) Note for details. For example, a press operator may need to perform a minor die cleaning task on a regular basis for product quality purposes and the use of safety blocks – inserted between the press dies – that are interlocked with the press electrical controls would constitute effective protection. Properly designed and applied safety block interlocks may be used in lieu of locking or tagging out the press's electrical energy source for purposes of the minor servicing exception.

Source: 29 CFR 1910.147(a)(2)(ii) Note.

---

## Training
Training is essential for employee protection. As an employer, you should:

- Train operators in safe mechanical press operation and hazardous energy control (lockout/tagout) procedures and techniques before they begin work on the press.
- Supervise operators to ensure that correct procedures and techniques are being followed.

## Additional Requirements
In addition, work practices such as regular mechanical power press inspection, maintenance, and reporting are essential.

- 29 CFR 1910.217(e)(1)(i) requires a program of periodic and regular inspections of mechanical power presses to ensure that all of the press parts, auxiliary equipment and safeguards are in safe operating condition and adjustment. Inspection certification records must be maintained.
- 29 CFR 1910.217(e)(1)(ii) requires you to inspect and test the condition of the clutch/brake mechanism, anti-repeat feature, and single-stroke mechanism on at least a weekly basis for presses without control reliability and brake system monitoring. Certification records must be maintained of these inspections and the maintenance performed.
- 29 CFR 1910.217(g)(1) requires the reporting of all point of operation injuries to operators or other employees within 30 days to either the Director of the Directorate of Standards and Guidance, OSHA, U.S. Department of Labor, Washington, DC 20210, or the state agency administering a plan approved by OSHA. You can also use the Internet to report injuries (www.osha.gov/pls/powerpress/mechanical.html).

---

### Applicable Standards

- 29 CFR 1910.147, *Control of hazardous energy (lockout/tagout).*
- 29 CFR 1910.217, *Mechanical power presses.*
- 29 CFR 1910.219, *Mechanical power-transmission apparatus.*

---

### Sources of Additional Information

- OSHA Instruction CPL 3-00-002 [CPL 2-1.35], *National Emphasis Program on Amputations*
- OSHA Publication 3067, *Concepts and Techniques of Machine Safeguarding* (http://www.osha.gov/Publications/Mach_Safeguard/toc.html)
- OSHA *Machine Guarding eTool* (http://www.osha.gov/SLTC/etools/machineguarding/index.html)
- *OSHA Lockout/Tagout Interactive Training Program* (http://www.osha.gov/dts/osta/lototraining/index.htm)
- NIOSH CIB 49, *Injuries and Amputations Resulting From Work with Mechanical Power Presses* (May 22, 1987)
- OSHA Instruction STD 01-12-021 [STD 1-12.21]—29 CFR 1910.217, *Mechanical Power Presses, Clarifications* (10/30/78)
- ANSI B11.1-2001, *Safety Requirements for Mechanical Power Presses*

## Power Press Brakes

Power press brakes are similar to mechanical power presses in that they use vertical reciprocating motion and are used for repetitive tasks. Press brake operation is either mechanical or hydraulic.

Press brakes are either general-purpose or special-purpose brakes, according to ANSI B11.3-2002, *Safety Requirements for Power Press Brakes.* General purpose press brakes have a single operator control station. A servo-system activates the special purpose brake, which may be equipped with multiple operator/helper control stations. (See *Figure 25* for a power press brake operation.)

**Figure 25  Power Press Brake Bending Metal**

## Hazards of Power Press Brakes

As with mechanical power presses, point of operation injuries are the most common type of injury associated with power press brakes. Here are some frequent causes of amputations from power press brakes:

- Foot controls being inadvertently activated while the operator's hand is in the point of operation. The likelihood of this type of injury increases as the size of stock decreases and brings the operator's hands closer to the point of operation.
- Parts of the body caught in pinch points created between the stock and the press brake frame while the bend is being made.
- Controls of a single-operator press bypassed by having a coworker activate the controls while

the operator positions or aligns stock or repairs or troubleshoots the press.
- Failure to properly lockout/tagout presses during the necessary tasks of making adjustments, clearing jams, performing maintenance, installing or aligning dies, or cleaning the machine.

---

**Case History #4**
An operator was bending small parts using an 80-ton unguarded press brake. This required the employee's fingers to be very close to the point of operation; and, consequently, the operator lost three fingers when his hand entered the point of operation. The operator on the previous shift had reported to the supervisor that the operator placed his fingers close to the point of operation, but was told that nothing could be done and that the operator should be careful.

**Case History #5**
An operator was bending metal parts using a 36-ton part-revolution power press brake that was foot-activated and equipped with a light curtain. About 3-4 inches of the light curtain had been "blanked out" during a previous part run. While adjusting a part at the point of operation, the employee accidentally activated the foot pedal and amputated three fingertips.

---

## Safeguarding Power Press Brakes

Primary safeguarding methods, such as physical guards and point of operation safeguarding devices (movable barrier devices, presence-sensing devices, pull-back devices, restraint devices, single- and two-hand devices) can be used to effectively guard power press brakes. (*Figure 26* shows a general-purpose power press brake used in conjunction with pullbacks.) Some safeguarding methods, such as presence-sensing devices, may require muting or blanking to allow the bending of material. Always ensure that these safety devices are properly installed, maintained, and used in accordance with the manufacturer's guidelines for the specific stock and task to be performed. Failure to do so could leave sensing field channels "blanked out" and expose operators to point-of-operation hazards as the safeguarding device's safety distance increases when blanking is used.

*Figure 26* Two-Person Power Press Brake Operation with Pullbacks

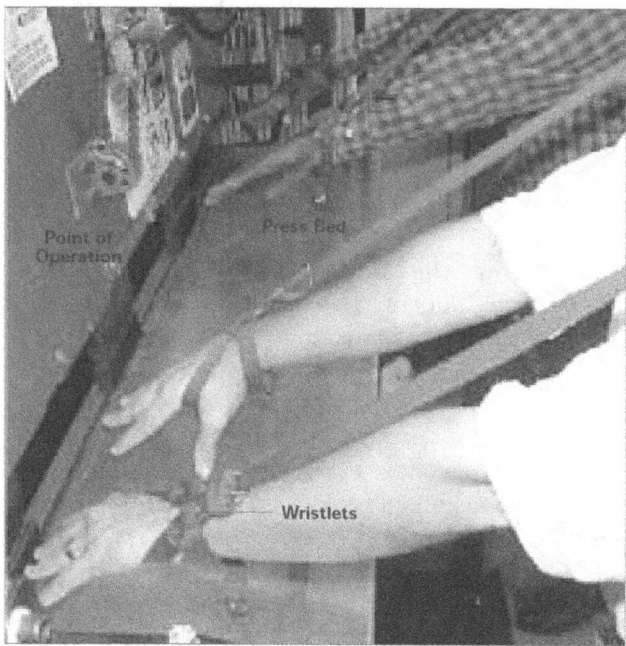

In other instances, such as with special-purpose power press brakes, machines are equipped with advanced control systems that are adaptable to all forms of safeguarding concepts and devices, such as two-hand controls and multiple operator/helper actuating controls. For example, *two-hand down, foot through (actuation)* methods are used to safeguard employees while they operate press brakes. With this safeguarding system, an operator uses a two-hand control to lower the press brake ram, for example, to within $1/4$ inch or less of the lower die (which is considered a safe opening). The operator then has the ability to maneuver and align the work-piece within this $1/4$ inch safe opening area and he or she is protected from the amputation hazard. Then the foot control is used by the operator to safely actuate the machine to produce the desired product.

Because of constraints imposed by certain manufacturing or fabricating processes, safeguarding by maintaining a *safe distance* from the point of operation may be acceptable. However, this is permitted only when safeguarding by barrier guard or safeguarding devices is not feasible (impossible) – that is, where the use of primary safeguarding method (such as a restraint device) is not feasible. Additional information about a *safe distance* safeguarding program can be found in OSHA Instruction 02-01-025 [CPL 2-1.25] – *Guidelines for Point of Operation Guarding of Power Press Brakes.*

## Other Controls for Power Press Brakes

The following are some secondary safeguarding methods and complementary equipment that may be used to supplement primary safeguarding or alone or in combination when primary safeguarding methods are not feasible:

- Safe distance safeguarding,
- Safe holding safeguarding,
- Safe work procedures,
- Work-holding equipment (such as back gauges),
- Properly designed and protected foot pedals, and
- Hand-feeding tools.

Ensure that proper safeguarding and lockout/tagout procedures are developed and implemented for power press brakes. Train and supervise employees in these procedures and conduct periodic inspections to ensure compliance.

---

### Applicable Standards

- 29 CFR 1910.147, *Control of hazardous energy (lockout/tagout).*
- 29 CFR 1910.212, *General requirements for all machines.*
- 29 CFR 1910.219, *Mechanical power-transmission apparatus.*

---

### Sources of Additional Information

- OSHA Publication 3067, *Concepts and Techniques of Machine Safeguarding* (http://www.osha.gov/Publications/Mach_Safeguard/toc.html)
- OSHA *Machine Guarding eTool* (http://www.osha.gov/SLTC/etools/machineguarding/index.html)
- *OSHA Lockout/Tagout Interactive Training Program* (http://www.osha.gov/dts/osta/lototraining/index.htm)
- OSHA Directive – CPL 02-01-025 [CPL 2-1.25], *Guidelines for Point of Operation Guarding of Power Press Brakes*
- ANSI B11.3-2002, *Safety Requirements for Power Press Brakes*

---

## Hazards of Conveyors

Conveyors are used in many industries to transport materials horizontally, vertically, at an angle, or around curves. Many conveyors have different and unique features and uses, so that hazards vary due to the material conveyed, the location of the conveyor, and the proximity of the conveyer to the employees. Types include unpowered and powered, live roller, slat, chain, screw, and pneumatic. Conveyors eliminate or reduce manual material handling tasks, but they present amputation hazards associated with mechanical motion. (See *Figures 27 through 30* for examples of common conveyors.)

Conveyor-related injuries typically involve a employee's hands or fingers becoming caught in nip points or shear points on conveyors and may occur in these situations:

• Cleaning and maintaining a conveyor, especially when it is still operating.
• Reaching into an in-going nip point to remove debris or to free jammed material.
• Allowing a cleaning cloth or an employee's clothing to get caught in the conveyor and pull the employee's fingers or hands into the conveyor.

Other conveyor-related hazards include improperly guarded gears, sprocket and chain drives, horizontal and vertical shafting, belts and pulleys, and power transmission couplings. Overhead conveyors warrant special attention because most of the conveyor's drive train is exposed. Employees have also been injured or killed while working in areas underneath conveyors and in areas around lubrication fittings, tension adjusters, and other equipment with hazardous energy sources.

**Case History #6**
While removing a cleaning rag from the ingoing nip point between the conveyor belt and its tail pulley (the unpowered end of the conveyor), an employee's arm became caught in the pulley, which amputated his arm below the elbow.

**Case History #7**
While servicing a chain-and-sprocket drive assembly on a roof tile conveyor system, an employee turned off the conveyor, removed the guard, and began work on the drive assembly without locking out the system. When someone started the conveyor, the employee's fingers became caught in the chain-and-sprocket drive and were amputated.

*Figure 27* **Belt Conveyor**

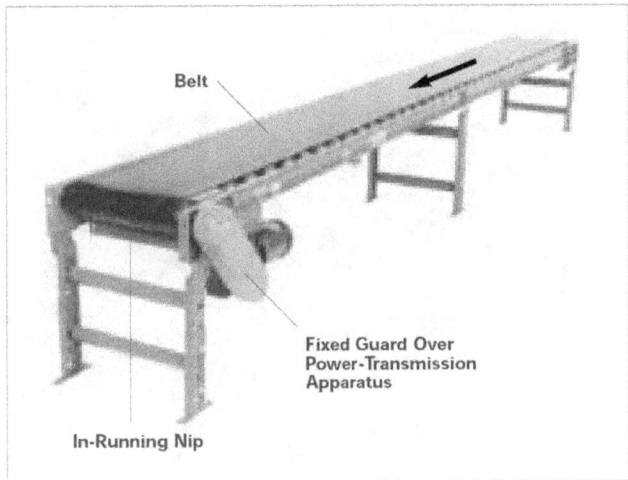

Belt

Fixed Guard Over Power-Transmission Apparatus

In-Running Nip

*Figure 28* **Screw Conveyor**

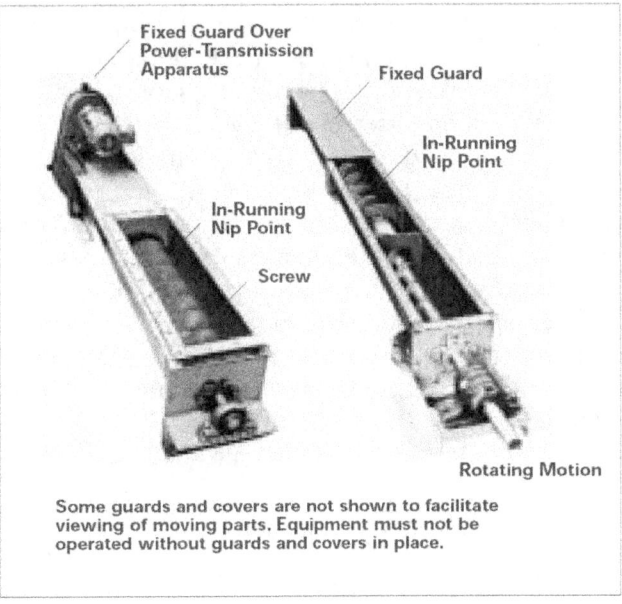

Fixed Guard Over Power-Transmission Apparatus

Fixed Guard

In-Running Nip Point

In-Running Nip Point

Screw

Rotating Motion

Some guards and covers are not shown to facilitate viewing of moving parts. Equipment must not be operated without guards and covers in place.

*Figure 29* **Chain Driven Live Roller Conveyor**

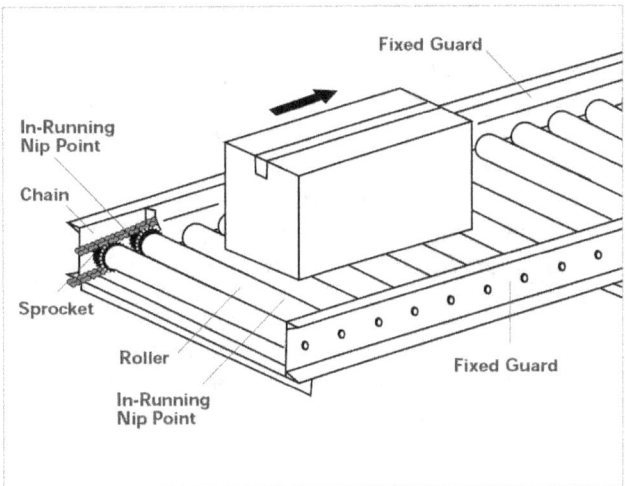

Fixed Guard

In-Running Nip Point

Chain

Sprocket

Roller

In-Running Nip Point

Fixed Guard

*Figure 30* Slat Conveyor

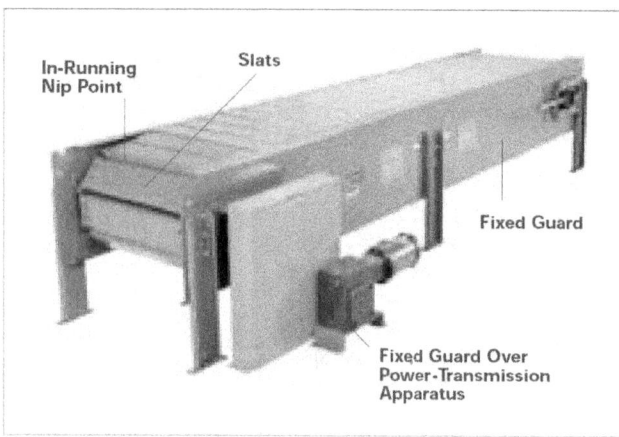

In-Running Nip Point
Slats
Fixed Guard
Fixed Guard Over Power-Transmission Apparatus

## Safeguarding Conveyors

As conveyor hazards vary depending on the application, employers need to look at each conveyor to evaluate and determine what primary safeguarding methods and energy control (lockout/tagout) practices are required. Where necessary for the protection of employees, conveyors need to have mechanical guards that protect the employee from nip points, shear points, and other moving parts, including power-transmission apparatus. Guards may include barriers, enclosures, grating, fences, or other obstructions that prevent inadvertent physical contact with operating machine components, such as point of operation areas, belts, gears, sprockets, chains, and other moving parts. A brief description of the hazards and recognized safeguarding methods is presented for common types of conveyors.

---

### Typical Conveyor Hazards and Safeguarding Methods

#### Belt Conveyors

*Hazards:* Belt-conveyor drive mechanisms and conveying mediums are hazardous as are the following belt-conveyor areas: 1) conveyor take-up and discharge ends; 2) where the belt or chain enters or exits the in-going nip point; 3) where the belt wraps around pulleys; 4) snub rollers where the belt changes direction, such as take-ups; 5) where multiple conveyors are adjoined; or 6) on transfers or deflectors used with belt conveyors.

*Controls:* The hazards associated with nip and shear points must be safeguarded. Side guards (spill guards), if properly designed can prevent employee contact with power-transmission component, in-going nip points and the conveying

---

medium. Secondary safeguarding methods for hazard control include the use of standard railings or fencing, or safeguarding by distance (location), and installing hazard awareness devices, such as pre-start-up signals and warning signs.

### Screw Conveyors

*Hazards:* Screw conveyors are troughs with a revolving longitudinal shaft on which a spiral or twisted plate is designed. In-going nip points, of turning helical flights for the entire length of the screw conveyor, exist between the revolving shaft and trough. Since the trough is not usually required to be covered for proper operation of the conveyor and because many screw conveyors are located at or near the floor level, the hazard of stepping into the danger area is ever present. Once caught, the victim is pulled further into the path of the conveying medium.

*Controls:* A screw conveyor housing must completely enclose the moving elements (screw mechanism, power transmission apparatus) of the conveyor, except for the loading and discharge points. Permanently affixed grids or polycarbonate can be installed for visibility purposes to allow the operator to inspect the operation. Alternatively, the trough side walls should be high enough to prevent employees from reaching over and falling into the trough. Open troughs can be used if covers are not feasible; but employees need to be protected by secondary safeguarding methods, such as a railing or fence.

Feed loading and discharge points can usually be guarded by providing enclosures, screening, grating, or some other interruption across the openings which will allow the passage of the material without allowing the entry of a part of the employee's body into the moving part(s).

### Chain Conveyors

*Hazards:* Nip points occur when a chain contacts a sprocket, such as when a chain runs around a sprocket or when the chain is supported by a sprocket or when a shoe above the chain precludes the chain from lifting off the sprocket. Nip points also occur at drives, terminals, take-ups (automatic take-ups may also have shear points), and idlers. Employee clothing, jewelry, and long hair may also get entangled and caught in the moving chain conveyor.

**Controls:** Sometimes, moving chains cannot be enclosed without impairing the functioning of the conveyor. However, in some cases, barrier guards may be installed around the moving parts for hazard enclosure purposes or, in other instances, nip and shear points may be eliminated by placing a guard at the nip point or shear point. Other secondary safeguarding options include safeguarding by distance (location) and the use of awareness devices.

### Roller Conveyors

**Hazards:** Roller conveyors are used to move material on a series of parallel rollers that are either powered or gravity-fed. Powered roller conveyors have the hazard of snagging and pulling objects, including hands, hair, and clothing into the area between the rollers and the stationary components of the conveyor. In-going nip points generally exist between the drive chain and sprockets; between belt and carrier rollers; and at terminals, drives, take-ups, idlers, and snub rollers.

**Controls:** Roller conveyors need to, where feasible, have permanent barrier guards that can be adjusted as necessary to protect the employee from nip and shear points. For example, the unused section of rollers closest to the employees needs to be guarded when transporting small items on a roller conveyor that do not require the use of the entire roller width. Also, conveyor hazards may be reduced by eliminating or minimizing projections from the roller and through the use of pop-up rollers. Other secondary safeguarding options include safeguarding by distance (location) and the use of awareness devices.

## Other Controls for Conveyors

The following are some secondary safeguarding methods, work practices, and complementary equipment that may be used to supplement primary safeguarding or alone or in combination when primary safeguarding methods are not feasible:

- Safeguarding by safe distance (by location) — locating moving parts away from employees to prevent accidental contact with the hazard point—is one option for safeguarding conveyors. It is particularly difficult, however, to use this method when employees need to be at or near unguarded moving parts.
- Use prominent awareness devices, such as warning signs or lights, to alert employees to the conveyor operation.
- Allow only trained individuals to operate conveyors and only trained, authorized staff to perform servicing and maintenance work.
- Visually inspect the entire conveyor and immediate work area prior to start-up to determine that the actuation will not cause an employee hazard.
- Inspect and test conveyor safety mechanisms, such as its alarms, emergency stops, and safeguarding methods.
- Do not use any conveyor which is unsafe until it is made safe.
- Forbid employees from riding on conveyors.
- Prohibit employees working with or near conveyors from wearing loose clothing or jewelry, and require them to secure long hair with a net or cap.
- Install emergency stop devices on conveyors where employees work when they cannot otherwise control the movement of the conveyor. This recognized safety feature provides employees with the means to shut off the equipment in the event of a hazardous situation or emergency incident.

For emergency stop devices, you will need these engineering controls:

- Equip conveyors with interlocking devices that shut them down during an electrical or mechanical overload such as product jam or other stoppage. Emergency devices need to be installed so that they cannot be overridden from other locations.
- When conveyors are arranged in a series, all should automatically stop whenever one stops.
- Equip conveyors with emergency stop controls that require manual resetting before resuming conveyor operation.
- Install clearly marked, unobstructed emergency stop buttons or pull cords within easy reach of employees.
- Provide continuously accessible conveyor belts with emergency stop cables that extend the entire length of the conveyor belt to allow access to the cable from any point along the belt.
- Ensure that conveyor controls or power sources can accept a lockout/tagout device to allow safe maintenance practices.

- Perform servicing and maintenance under an energy control program in accordance with the *Control of hazardous energy (lockout/tagout)*, 29 CFR 1910.147, standard. For example, instruct employees to lubricate, align, service, and maintain conveyors when the conveyor is locked or tagged out if the task would expose them to an area of the conveyor (or adjacent machinery) where hazardous energy exists.

---

### Minor Servicing

At times, OSHA recognizes that some minor servicing may have to be performed during normal production operations, so a lockout/tagout exception is allowed. See the 29 CFR 1910.147(a)(2)(ii) Note for details. An example of a common conveyor minor servicing activity involves package jams where an employee must frequently dislodge the jam. To prevent unexpected start-up of the conveyor, employers may adopt alternative control measures, such as opening (placing in the off position) local disconnects or control switches to prevent conveyor start-up. These properly applied devices, if used, must be under the exclusive control of the employee performing the jam release, so that no other person can restart the conveyor without the knowledge and consent of the person performing the servicing work.

Source: 29 CFR 1910.147(a)(2)(ii) Note.

---

### Applicable Standards

- 29 CFR 1910.147, *Control of hazardous energy (lockout/tagout)*.
- 29 CFR 1910.212, *General requirements for all machines*.
- 29 CFR 1910.219, *Mechanical power-transmission apparatus*.
- 29 CFR 1910.269, *Electric power generation, transmission and distribution* [as detailed in section (v)(11)].
- 29 CFR 1926.555, *Conveyors*.
- ANSI B20.1-57, *Safety Code for Conveyors, Cableways, and Related Equipment* – as incorporated by reference in 1910.218(j)(3), 1910.261(a)(3)(x), 1910.261(b)(1), 1910.261(c)(15)(iv), 1910.261(f)(4), 1910.261(j)(2), 1910.265(c)(18)(i)].

---

### Sources of Additional Information

- OSHA Publication 3067, *Concepts and Techniques of Machine Safeguarding* (http://www.osha.gov/Publications/Mach_Safeguard/toc.html)
- OSHA *Machine Guarding eTool* (http://www.osha.gov/SLTC/etools/machineguarding/index.html)
- *OSHA Lockout/Tagout Interactive Training Program* (http://www.osha.gov/dts/osta/lototraining/index.htm)
- ASME B20.1-2003, *Safety Standard for Conveyors and Related Equipment*.
- ANSI/CEMA 350-2003, *Screw Conveyors*.
- ANSI/CEMA 401-2003, *Unit Handling Conveyors—Roller Conveyors—Non-powered*.
- ANSI/CEMA 402-2003, *Unit Handling Conveyors—Belt Conveyors*.
- *ANSI/CEMA 403-2003, Unit Handling Conveyors—Belt Driven Live Roller Conveyors*.
- ANSI/CEMA 404-2003, *Unit Handling Conveyors—Chain Driven Live Roller Conveyors*.
- ANSI/CEMA 405-2003, *Package Handling Conveyors—Slat Conveyors*

## Hazards of Printing Presses

Printing presses vary by type and size, ranging from relatively simple manual presses to the complex large presses used for printing newspapers, magazines, and books. Printing presses are often part of a larger system that also includes cutting, binding, folding, and finishing equipment. Many modern printing presses rely on computer controls, and the high speeds of such equipment often require rapid machine adjustments to avoid waste.

This section discusses amputation hazards associated with two common types of printing presses: web-fed and sheet-fed printing press systems. Web-fed printing presses are fed by large continuous rolls of substrate such as paper, fabric or plastic; sheet-fed printing presses, as their name implies, are fed by large sheets of substrate. In both types, the substrate typically feeds through a series of cylinders containing printing plates and supporting cylinders moving in the opposite direction. (*Figures 31 and 32* illustrate a roll-to-roll offset printing press and a sheet-fed offset printing press.)

*Figure 31* Roll-to-Roll Offset Printing Press

*Figure 32* Sheet-Fed Offset Printing Press

As with other machines, printing press-related amputations occur during servicing and maintenance activities. For example, amputations occur when employees get their fingers or hands caught in the in-going nip points created between two rollers while:

- Hand-feeding the leading edge of paper into the in-running rollers during press set-up while the machine is operating;
- Adjusting ink flow on a press;
- Cleaning ink off the press while it is operating;
- Attempting to free material from the rollers;
- Straightening misaligned sheets of paper in the press;
- Jogging the printer and making adjustments to the equipment (such as adjusting the nip wheel on a sheeter);
- Using rags to clean machinery adjacent to unguarded rollers.

Source: OSHA IMIS Accident Investigation Database.

## Safeguarding Printing Presses

As with most machinery, you can rely on primary safeguarding methods to protect employees against injuries when using printing presses. For example, some primary safeguarding methods include the following:

- Install guards on all mechanical hazard points that are accessible during normal operation -- such as accessible in-going nip points between rollers and power-transmission apparatus (chains and sprockets).
- Safeguard nip point hazards with barrier guards or nip guards. Nip guards need to be designed and installed without creating additional hazards.
- Install fixed barrier guards, with tamper-proof fasteners, at rollers that do not require operator access.
- Properly designed, applied, and maintained safeguarding devices (such as presence-sensing devices and mats) may also be used to keep your body out of machine danger areas. However, these control circuit devices are no substitute for lockout/tagout.
- Use hold-to-run controls (such as inch or reverse) that protect employees from machine mechanical hazards by either: 1) requiring the use of both hands for control initiation purposes; or 2) are mounted at a safe distance so that an employee cannot inch or reverse the press

and simultaneously access any unguarded danger area or otherwise reach into the danger zone while the press is operating.

## Other Controls for Printing Presses

The following are some secondary safeguarding methods, work practices, and complementary equipment that may be used to supplement primary safeguarding or alone or in combination when primary safeguarding methods are not feasible:

- Make sure that printing presses attended by more than one operator or ones outside of the operator's viewing area are equipped with visual and audible warning devices to alert employees regarding the press's operational status—in operation, safe mode, or impending operation.
- Install visual warning devices of sufficient number and brightness and locate them so that they are readily visible to press personnel.
- Ensure that audible alarms are loud enough to be heard above background noise.
- Provide a warning system that activates for at least 2 seconds prior to machine motion.
- Use additional secondary safeguarding methods such as safeguarding by location and safe work (operating) procedures for printing presses.
- Ensure that all press operators receive appropriate training and supervision until they can work safely on their own.
- Prohibit employees working with or near printing presses from wearing loose clothing or jewelry and require them to secure long hair with a net or cap.
- Conduct periodic inspections to ensure compliance.
- Perform servicing and maintenance under an energy control program in accordance with the *Control of hazardous energy (lockout/tagout)*, 29 CFR 1910.147, standard.

### Minor Servicing

At times, OSHA recognizes that some minor servicing may have to be performed during normal production operations, so a lockout/tagout exception is allowed. See the 29 CFR 1910.147(a)(2)(ii) Note for details. Minor servicing can include, among other things, tasks such as clearing of certain types of minor paper jams; minor cleaning; minor lubricating and minor adjusting operations; certain plate and blanket changing

tasks; and, in some cases, paper webbing and paper roll changing. Generally speaking, minor servicing is considered to include those tasks involving operations that can be safely accomplished by employees and where extensive disassembly of equipment is not required.

One such control method that does offer effective alternative protection is the inch-safe-service technique when it is used in conjunction with the main drive control. This technique is specified in the American National Standards (ANSI B65.1 and ANSI B65.2) for web- and sheet-fed printing presses and binding and finishing equipment, respectively.

Also, interlock guards and presence-sensing safeguarding devices, if properly designed, applied and maintained, would also be considered effective protection. For example, you could simply open the barrier guard and rely on the protection afforded by the properly designed interlock control circuit while clearing minor paper jams and other minor servicing functions that occur using normal production operations and which meet the criteria in the lockout/tagout exception.

Source: 29 CFR 1910.147(a)(2)(ii) Note.

### Applicable Standards

- 29 CFR 1910.147, Control of hazardous energy (lockout/tagout).
- 29 CFR 1910.212, General requirements for all machines.
- 29 CFR 1910.219, Mechanical power-transmission apparatus.

### Sources of Additional Information

- OSHA Publication 3067, *Concepts and Techniques of Machine Safeguarding* (http://www.osha.gov/Publications/Mach_Safeguard/toc.html)
- OSHA *Machine Guarding eTool* (http://www.osha.gov/SLTC/etools/machineguarding/index.html)
- *OSHA Lockout/Tagout Interactive Training Program* (http://www.osha.gov/dts/osta/lototraining/index.htm)
- ANSI B65.1-2005, *Safety Standard - Printing Press Systems*

## Hazards of Roll-Forming and Roll-Bending Machines

Roll-forming and roll-bending machines primarily perform metal bending, rolling, or shaping functions. Roll-forming is the process of bending a continuous strip of metal to gradually form a predetermined shape using a self-contained machine. Roll-forming machines contain a series of rolls that may or may not have braking systems. Roll-forming machines may also perform other processes on the metal, including piercing holes, slots, or notches; stamping; flanging; and stretch-bending. Roll-bending machines usually have three rolls arranged like a pyramid and they perform essentially the same process as roll-forming, except that the machine produces a bend across the width of flat or pre-formed metal to achieve a curved or angular configuration.

Roll-forming and roll-bending machines frequently are set up and operated by one person. (*Figure 33* illustrates a roll-forming machine producing a finished product. *Figure 34* illustrates the in-feed section of a roll-forming machine.)

*Figure 33* **Roll-Forming Machine**

*Figure 34* **In-Feed Area of a Roll-Forming Machine**

The most common type of amputation hazard associated with roll-forming and roll-bending machines are point of operation hazards created by in-running nip points. Amputations occur when the hands of the operator feeding material through the rolls get caught and are then pulled into the point of operation. Causes of amputations related to roll-forming and roll-bending machines can occur from the following:

- Having an unguarded or inadequately guarded point of operation;
- Locating the operator control station too close to the process;
- Activating the machine inadvertently; and
- Performing cleaning, clearing, changing, or inspecting tasks while the machine is operating or is not properly locked or tagged out.

---

**Case History #10**
While feeding a metal sheet into a roller, an employee caught his right hand in the roller and amputated one finger.

**Case History #11**
An employee wearing gloves caught his left hand in a roll-forming machine, resulting in partial amputation of two fingers. The employee was standing close to the moving rollers, feeding flat steel sheet from behind and catching it on the front side. There was no point of operation guard on the front roller and the foot operating pedal was very close to the machine.

---

## Safeguarding Roll-Forming and Roll-Bending Machines

Roll-forming and roll-bending machines are available in a wide variety of sizes and designs, and safeguarding methods must be tailored for each machine. Several factors affect the ways to safeguard the equipment, including whether a machine has a brake system, its size, operating speed, thickness of product, length of production runs, required production accuracy, sheet feeding methods, and part removal methods. Depending on the size and type of machine, a number of different primary safeguarding methods may be required to adequately protect the operator as well as other employees nearby. For example, you can do the following:

- Install fixed or adjustable point of operation barrier guards at the in-feed and out-feed sections of machines. If the stock or end-product does not differ greatly from run to run, a fixed guard may be preferable. If the stock or end-product is variable, however, an adjustable guard may be more suitable.

- Install fixed point of operation guards to cover the sides of the rollers to prevent entry of clothing and parts of your body into the in-going nip points of the rollers.
- Install fixed or interlocked guards to cover any other rotating parts, such as power-transmission apparatus.
- Install and use properly applied presence-sensing safeguarding devices (light curtains, safety mats) on roll-forming and roll-bending machines (those equipped with brakes) to protect you from hazardous machine areas during normal production operations.
- Install and use properly applied two-hand control safeguarding devices to protect you from the machine hazards during roll-bending production operations.
- Ensure that operators use the jog mode during feeding operations, if appropriate, and that the control station requires the use of both hands or is mounted at a safe distance from the machine's danger areas.
- Allow only one control station to operate at any one time when a single machine has more than one set of operator controls. This does not apply to the emergency stop controls, which must be operable from all locations at all times, such as accessible in-going nip points between rollers and power-transmission apparatus (chains and sprockets).

## Other Controls for Roll-Forming and Roll-Bending Machines

The following are some secondary safeguarding methods, work practices, and complementary equipment that may be used to supplement primary safeguarding or alone or in combination when primary safeguarding methods are not feasible:

- Use proper lighting and awareness barrier devices (such as interlocking gates around the perimeter of the machine to prevent unauthorized entry), awareness signals and signs.
- Position (safeguard by location) operating stations in a way that ensures that operators are not exposed to the machine's point of operation.
- Locate foot pedal controls away from the point of operation and guard them in such a way as to prevent inadvertent activation. Some foot controls use dead-man (hold-to-run) features so that

the rolls stop turning (via a brake and clutch assembly) when you release the foot switch.
- Develop and implement safe work (operating) procedures for roll-forming and roll-bending machines.
- Safeguard operator control stations to prevent inadvertent activation by unauthorized employees.
- Ensure that all operators receive appropriate on-the-job training under the direct supervision of experienced operators until they can work safely on their own.
- Prohibit employees working with or near printing presses from wearing loose clothing or jewelry and require them to secure long hair with a net or cap.
- Install safety trip controls, such as a pressure-sensitive body bar or safety tripwire cable, on the in-feed section of the machine to shut down the machine if an employee gets too close to the point of operation.
- Install emergency stop controls that are readily accessible to the operator.
- Conduct periodic inspections to ensure compliance.
- Perform servicing and maintenance under an energy control program in accordance with the *Control of hazardous energy (lockout/tagout)*, 29 CFR 1910.147, standard.

---

### Applicable Standards

- 29 CFR 1910.147, *Control of hazardous energy (lockout/tagout)*.
- 29 CFR 1910.212, *General requirements for all machines*.
- 29 CFR 1910.219, *Mechanical power-transmission apparatus*.

---

### Sources of Additional Information

- OSHA Publication 3067, *Concepts and Techniques of Machine Safeguarding* (http://www.osha.gov/Publications/Mach_Safeguard/toc.html)
- OSHA *Machine Guarding eTool* (http://www.osha.gov/SLTC/etools/machineguarding/index.html)
- *OSHA Lockout/Tagout Interactive Training Program* (http://www.osha.gov/dts/osta/lototraining/index.htm)
- ANSI B11.12-2005, *Safety Requirements for Roll-Forming and Roll-Bending Machines*

## Hazards of Shearing Machines

Mechanical power shears contain a ram for their shearing action. The ram moves a non-rotary blade at a constant rate past the edge of a fixed blade. Shears may be mechanically, hydraulically, hydra-mechanically, pneumatically, or manually powered and are used to perform numerous functions such as squaring, cropping, and cutting to length.

In the basic shear operation, stock is fed into the point of operation between two blades. A hold-down may then be activated that applies pressure to the stock to prevent movement. One complete cycle consists of a downward stroke of the top blade until it passes the lower fixed blade followed by an upward stroke to the starting position. (See *Figures 35 and 36* for examples of alligator and power squaring shears.)

*Figure 35* **Hydraulic Alligator Shear**

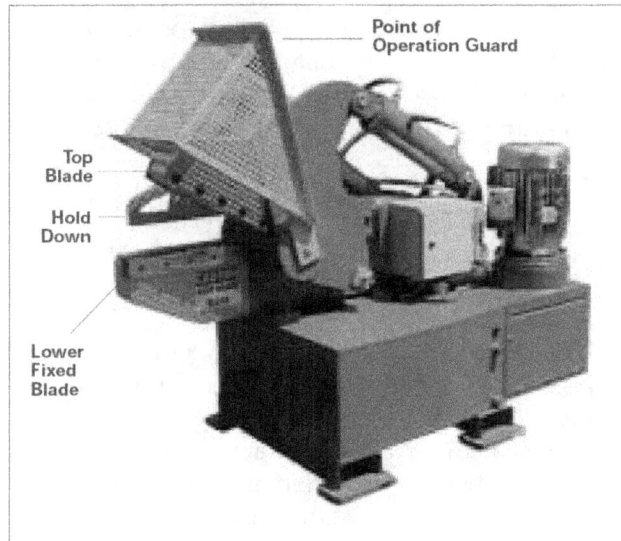

*Figure 36* **Power Squaring Shear**

**Shears can be categorized as stand-alone manual shears, stand-alone automatic shears, and process-line shears.**

**Stand-alone manual shears.** An operator controls them from a control station. The operator feeds the shear either by hand or by activating the automatic loading mechanism and activates the equipment using hand or foot controls or a tripping device on the back side of the shear. An example is an alligator shear.

**Stand-alone automatic shears.** These feed and stroke automatically and continuously. The operator uses hand-activated or foot-activated controls to initiate the operation, which requires limited additional operator interaction. An example is a guillotine shear.

**Process-line shears.** These are integrated into an automated production process and are controlled automatically as part of the process. Examples include crop shears and cut-to-length shears.

The two primary point-of-operation hazards on shears are the shear blade and the material hold-downs. Amputations may occur in the following situations:

- The foot control inadvertently activates while the operator's hands are in the point of operation. Such amputations usually relate to foot-activated, stand-alone manual shears that require the use of both hands to feed the stock.
- A tripping device located on the back side of the shear's mouth operates the shear but does not prevent the operator from reaching into the hazard area. Such tripping devices, commonly found on stand-alone manual shears, may increase productivity but must be used in conjunction with primary safeguards.
- When there is no hold-down and stock being fed into a stand-alone manual shear kicks out and strikes the operator's hands or fingers.

### Case History #12

After breaking metal with a mechanical alligator shear, an employee turned the shear off and was picking up debris on the ground when he placed his left hand on the shear and amputated his fingers. The shear's flywheel was not equipped with a clutch or similar device. So, when the shear was shut off, the jaw continued to operate on stored energy.

## Safeguarding Shearing Machines

Because shears have a wide variety of applications, safeguarding methods must be determined individually for each machine based on its use. A number of different safeguarding methods may be necessary to adequately protect the operator as well as other employees nearby. For example, you will need to consider the machine size, operating speed, size and type of material, length of production runs, required accuracy of the work, methods for material feeding and removal, operator controls, and clutch type.

Here are some primary safeguarding options for protecting employees from the shear's point of operation during feeding activities at the front of the machine:

- Install a properly applied fixed or adjustable point of operation guard at the in-feed of the shearing machine to prevent operator contact with the shear's point of operation as well as the pinch point of the hold-down. The guard's design must prevent the employee from reaching under or around it.
- Install and arrange two-hand trips and controls so that the operator must use both hands to initiate the shear cycle. Two-hand trips and controls need to be designed so that they cannot be defeated easily. The Safety Requirements for Shears (ANSI B11.4-2003) standard recommends the installation of additional safeguarding when two-hand controls are used on part-revolution shears, based on the nature of the shearing operation. This national consensus standard specifies the use of guards on full-revolution shears.
- Use a properly applied presence-sensing device, such as a light curtain, on shears that are hydraulically powered or equipped with a part-revolution clutch.

- Mount guarded foot-pedal controls at a safe distance (single control safeguarding devices) away from the point of operation to protect the operator during the operating cycle.
- Use pull-backs or restraints for stand-alone manual shears when other guarding methods are not feasible or do not adequately protect employees. (These devices may not be appropriate if the job requires employees' mobility.)
- Use automatic-feeding devices such as conveyors with stand-alone manual shears when the material is uniform in size and shape.
- Equip mechanical shears with either a part-revolution or full-revolution clutch. Methods of safeguarding depend on the type of clutch in use. Shears equipped with full-revolution clutches used in single-stroke operations must be equipped with an anti-repeat feature.

## Other Controls for Shearing Machines

The following are some secondary safeguarding methods, work practices, and complementary equipment that may be used to supplement primary safeguarding or alone or in combination when primary safeguarding methods are not feasible:

- Install guarded operating stations at a safe distance (safeguarding by location) from the shear's point of operation to prevent inadvertent activation.
- Develop and implement safe work (operating) procedures for shearing machines and conduct periodic inspections to ensure compliance.
- Use proper lighting and awareness devices, such as awareness barriers and warning signs, to warn employees of the hazard.
- Install hold-down (work-holding) devices that prevent the work piece from kicking up and striking the operator. Hold-down devices may eliminate the need for employees to hold the material near the point of operation.
- Instruct operators to use distancing tools when their hands might otherwise reach into the point of operation because of the size of the material being cut.
- Where it is possible to stop the shear during its operating cycle, install an emergency stop device—such as a pressure-sensitive body bar, safety tripod, or safety tripwire cable—at the in-feed section of the shear.
- Install an awareness barrier or a safety trip control (safety tripwire or safety tripod) on the back side of the shear.
- Ensure that all operators receive on-the-job

training under the direct supervision of experienced operators until they can work safely on their own.

- Instruct employees to perform routine maintenance on the clutch and braking systems.
- Instruct employees to inspect all guarding to ensure that it is in place properly before the machine is operated.
- Instruct supervisors to ensure that operators keep their hands out of the shear's point of operation at all times while the machine is energized and not properly locked out.
- Instruct employees not to perform activities on the back side of a shear while it is operating or still energized.
- Prohibit employees from riding the foot activation pedal.
- Perform servicing and maintenance under an energy control program in accordance with the *Control of hazardous energy (lockout/tagout)*, 29 CFR 1910.147, standard.

---

**Applicable Standards**

- 29 CFR 1910.212, *General requirements for all machines*
- 29 CFR 1910.219, *Mechanical power-transmission apparatus*
- 29 CFR 1910.147, *Control of hazardous energy (lockout/tagout)*

---

**Sources of Additional Information**

- OSHA Instruction CPL 03-00-002, *National Emphasis Program on Amputations.*
- OSHA Publication 3067, *Concepts and Techniques of Machine Safeguarding* (http://www.osha.gov/Publications/Mach_Safeguard/toc.html)
- OSHA *Machine Guarding eTool* (http://www.osha.gov/SLTC/etools/machineguarding/index.html)
- *OSHA Lockout/Tagout Interactive Training Program* (http://www.osha.gov/dts/osta/lototraining/index.htm)
- ANSI B11.4-2003, *Safety Requirements for Shears.*

---

## Hazards of Food Slicers

Food slicers are electrically powered machines typically equipped with a rotary blade, an on/off switch, thickness adjustment, and a food holder or chute. A pushing/guarding device or plunger may be used to apply pressure to the food against the slicer blade, or pressure may be applied by gravity and/or by an attachment connected to the food holder. (See *Figure 37.*)

**Figure 37** Meat Slicer

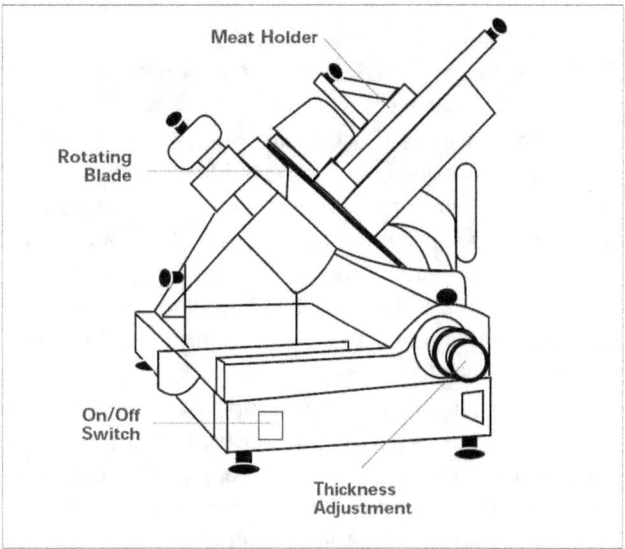

Amputations resulting from work with food slicers can occur as follows:

- When the operator adjusts or services the slicer while it is still operating or while it is switched off but still plugged in, or energized. In the latter case, amputations occur when the operator accidentally switches the slicer on.
- When the operator fails to use the sliding attachment on the food-holding device, especially when slicing small pieces of meat.
- When the operator hand-feeds food into a chute-fed slicer without using the proper pushing/guarding device or plunger.

---

**Case History #14**
Two employees, an operator and an assistant, were using a meat slicer to slice turkey. The assistant was holding a box of turkey in a tilted position while the operator fed the turkey into the slicer. The operator removed the guard from the meat slicer because the turkey kept jamming. The slicer's knives caught the operator's glove and pulled his hand into the knives, amputating his finger just above the nail.

---

## Safeguarding and Other Controls for Food Slicers

Food slicers must be used with guards that cover the unused portions of the slicer blade on both the top and bottom of the slicer. You should buy slicers already equipped with a feeding attachment on the sliding mechanism of the food holder or purchase the attachment separately and install it before use. Instruct employees to use a pushing/guarding device with chute-fed slicers.

The following are some secondary safeguarding methods, work practices and complementary equipment that may be used to supplement primary safeguarding or alone or in combination when primary safeguarding methods are not feasible:

- Develop and implement safe work (operating) procedures for slicers and conduct periodic inspections to ensure compliance.
- Ensure that all operators receive on-the-job training under the direct supervision of experienced operators until they can work safely on their own.
- Use warning signs to alert employees of the hazard and safety instructions.
- Instruct operators to use plungers to feed food into chute-fed slicers. For other slicers, they should use the feeding attachment located on the food-holder.
- Never place food into the slicer by hand-feeding or hand pressure.
- Instruct operators to retract the slicer blade during cleaning operations.
- Instruct operators to turn off and unplug slicers when not in use or when left unattended for any period of time.
- Perform servicing and maintenance under an energy control program in accordance with the *Control of hazardous energy (lockout/tagout)*, 29 CFR 1910.147, standard. You can avoid slicer lockout/tagout if the equipment is cord-and-plug connected equipment simply by having exclusive control over the attachment plug after you shut the slicer off and unplug it from the energy source.

## Hazards of Meat Grinders

Electric meat grinders typically have a feeding tray attached to a tubular throat, a screw auger that pushes meat to the cutting blade and through the cutting plate, an on/off switch, a reverse switch, and a plunger. (See *Figure 38.*)

*Figure 38*  Stainless Steel Meat Grinder

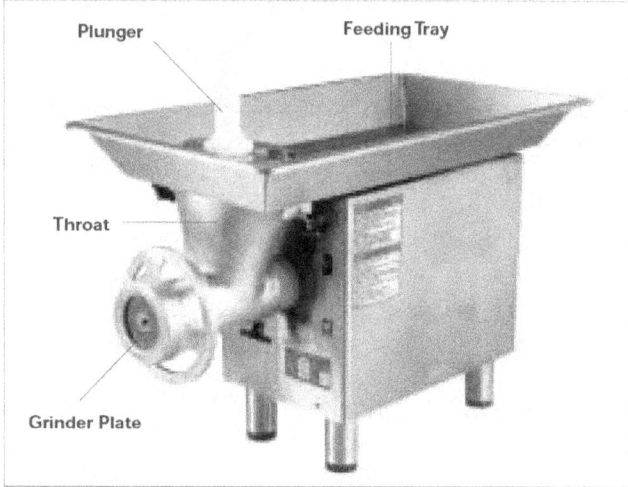

Amputations can occur when:

- The operator reaches into the throat of the grinder while it is still operating or while it is switched off but still plugged in (energized). In the latter case, amputations can occur when the operator accidentally switches the grinder back on.
- The operator fails to use the attached feeding tray and throat.

Defective meat grinders, such as ones with holes in the throat or screw auger area, are also a source of workplace amputations and must be taken out of service.

she reassembled it. Also, she did not use the plunger provided for feeding the meat into the grinder. The machine pulled her hand into the 3-inch diameter auger and amputated it above the wrist.

Source: OSHA IMIS Accident Investigation Database.

## Safeguarding and Other Controls for Meat Grinders

Meat grinders must be retrofitted with a primary safeguard, such as a properly designed tapered throat or fixed guard, in cases where the machine design is such that an employee's hand may come in contact with the point-of-operation (that is the auger cutter area). You should buy meat grinders already equipped with this primary safeguard.

The following are some other secondary safeguarding methods, work practices, and complementary equipment that may be used to supplement primary safeguarding or alone or in combination when primary safeguarding methods are not feasible:

- Develop and implement safe work (operating) procedures for meat grinders to ensure that the guards are adequate and in place, and that the grinder feeding methods are performed safely. Conduct periodic inspections of grinder operations to ensure compliance.
- Use warning signs to alert employees of the hazard and safety instructions.
- Ensure that all operators receive appropriate on-the-job training under direct supervision of experienced operators until they can work safely on their own.
- Provide operators with properly sized plungers to eliminate the need for their hands to enter the feed throat during operation.
- Instruct operators to use the proper plunger device to feed meat into grinders. No other device should be used to feed the grinder.
- Instruct employees to operate grinders only with feeding trays and throats installed.
- Instruct operators to use the meat grinder only for its intended purpose.
- Instruct operators to turn off and unplug grinders when not in use or when left unattended for any period of time.
- Perform servicing and maintenance under an energy control program in accordance with the

Control of hazardous energy (lockout/tagout), 29 CFR 1910.147, standard. You can avoid slicer lockout/tagout if the equipment is cord-and-plug connected equipment simply by having exclusive control over the attachment plug after you shut the slicer off and unplug it from the energy source.

### Applicable Standards

- 29 CFR 1910.147, Control of hazardous energy (lockout/tagout).
- 29 CFR 1910.212, General requirements for all machines.
- 29 CFR 1910.219, Mechanical power-transmission apparatus.

### Sources of Additional Information

- OSHA Instruction CPL 03-00-002, National Emphasis Program on Amputations.
- OSHA Publication 3067, Concepts and Techniques of Machine Safeguarding (http://www.osha.gov/Publications/Mach_Safeguard/toc.html)
- OSHA Machine Guarding eTool (http://www.osha.gov/SLTC/etools/machineguarding/index.html)
- OSHA Lockout/Tagout Interactive Training Program (http://www.osha.gov/dts/osta/lototraining/index.htm)

## Hazards of Meat-Cutting Band Saws

Band saws can cut wood, plastic, metal, or meat. These saws use a thin, flexible, continuous steel strip with cutting teeth on one edge that runs around two large motorized pulleys or wheels. The blade runs on two pulleys (driver and idler) and passes through a hole in the work table where the operator feeds the stock. Blades are available with various teeth sizes, and the saws usually have adjustable blade speeds.

Unlike band saws used in other industries, meat-cutting band saws are usually constructed of stainless steel for sanitary purposes and for easy cleaning. The table, which may slide or roll, has a pushing guard installed to protect the operator while feeding the saw. Meat-cutting band saws may also be equipped with a fence and pushing guard to feed the meat through the band saw. (See Figure 39.)

*Figure 39*  Stainless Steel Meat-Cutting Band Saw

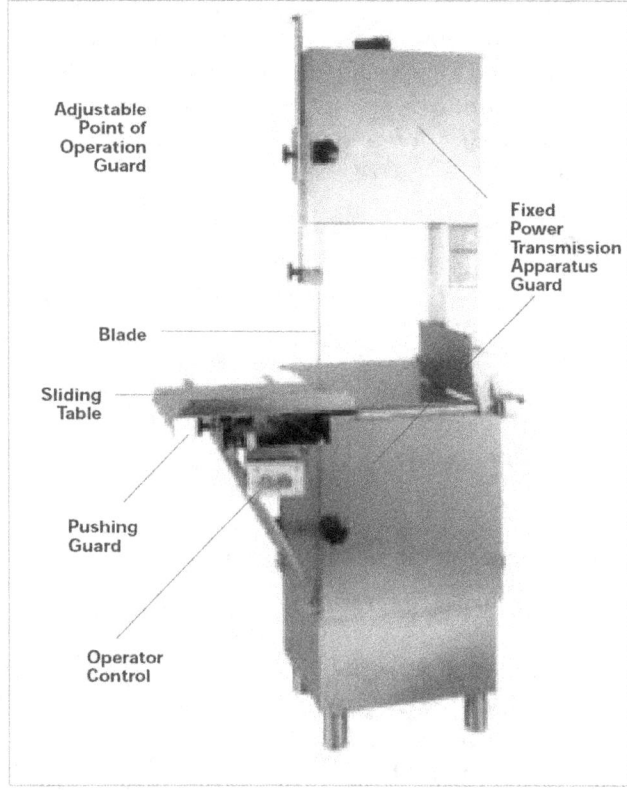

Adjustable Point of Operation Guard

Fixed Power Transmission Apparatus Guard

Blade

Sliding Table

Pushing Guard

Operator Control

Amputations occur most frequently when operators' hands contact the running saw blade while feeding meat into the saw. The risk of amputation is greatest when operators place their hands too close to the saw blade, in a direct line with the saw blade, or beneath the adjustable guard during feeding operations. Here are some common causes of amputations involving meat-cutting band saws:

• The operator's hand slips off the meat or otherwise accidentally runs through the blade.
• The operator attempts to remove meat from the band saw table while the blade is still moving.
• The operator's gloves, jewelry, or loose-fitting clothing became entangled in the saw blade.

**Case History #18**
While operating a band saw to cut pork loin, an employee amputated his right index finger when his hand slipped and contacted the moving blade.

**Case History #19**
An operator amputated the tip of his right ring finger while using a band saw to cut ¼-inch slabs of meat from a 4-inch thick piece of beef. As the piece of meat got smaller, his hands

moved too close to the saw blade. The employee was not using the pusher guard provided for the saw.

Source: OSHA IMIS Accident Investigation Database.

## Safeguarding and Other Controls for Meat-Cutting Band Saws

Primary safeguarding methods that you can use include the following:

• Install a self-adjusting guard over the entire blade, except at the working portion, or point of operation of the blade.  The guard must be adjustable to cover the unused portion of the blade above the meat during cutting operations.
• Enclose the pulley mechanism and motor completely.

The following are some secondary safeguarding methods, work practices, and complementary equipment that may be used to supplement primary safeguarding or alone or in combination when primary safeguarding methods are not feasible:

• Develop and implement safe work (operating) procedures for meat-cutting band saws to ensure that the guards are adequate and in place and that operators safely perform feeding methods.
• Ensure that all operators receive adequate on-the-job training under the direct supervision of experienced operators until they can work safely on their own.
• Use warning signs to alert employees of the hazard and safety instructions.
• Install a brake on one or both wheels to prevent the saw blade from coasting after the machine is shut off.
• Provide a pushing guard or fence to feed meat into the saw blade.
• Instruct operators to use the pushing guard or fence to feed the saw, especially when cutting small pieces of meat.
• Instruct operators to adjust the point of operation guard properly to fit the thickness of the meat.
• Instruct operators to use only sharp meat-cutting blades and to tighten blades to the appropriate tension with the machine's tension control device.

- Instruct operators not to wear gloves, jewelry, or loose-fitting clothing while operating a band saw and to secure long hair in a net or cap.
- Prohibit operators from removing meat from the band saw while the saw blade is still moving.
- Instruct operators to turn off and unplug band saws when not in use or when left unattended for any period of time.
- Conduct periodic inspections of the saw operation to ensure compliance.
- Perform servicing and maintenance under an energy control program in accordance with the *Control of hazardous energy (lockout/tagout)*, 29 CFR 1910.147, standard. You can avoid slicer lockout/tagout if the equipment is cord-and-plug connected equipment simply by having exclusive control over the attachment plug after you shut the band saw off and unplug it from the energy source.

### Applicable Standards

- 29 CFR 1910.147, *Control of hazardous energy (lockout/tagout)*.
- 29 CFR 1910.212, *General requirements for all machines*.
- 29 CFR 1910.219, *Mechanical power-transmission apparatus*.

### Sources of Additional Information

- OSHA Publication 3067, *Concepts and Techniques of Machine Safeguarding* (http://www.osha.gov/Publications/Mach_Safeguard/toc.html)
- OSHA *Machine Guarding eTool* (http://www.osha.gov/SLTC/etools/machineguarding/index.html)
- *OSHA Lockout/Tagout Interactive Training Program* (http://www.osha.gov/dts/osta/lototraining/index.htm)
- OSHA Publication 3157, *A Guide for Protecting Workers from Woodworking Hazards* (http://www.osha.gov/Publication/osha3157.pdf)

## Hazards of Drill Presses

Electric drill presses use a rotating bit to drill or cut holes in wood or metal. The holes may be cut to a desired preset depth or completely through the stock. A basic drill press operation consists of selecting an appropriate drill bit, tightening the bit in the chuck, setting the drill depth, placing the

material on the drill press bed, securing the work to the bed so that it will not rotate during drilling, turning the drill press on, and pulling the drill press lever down so that the drill bit will be lowered into the stock. (See *Figure 40*.)

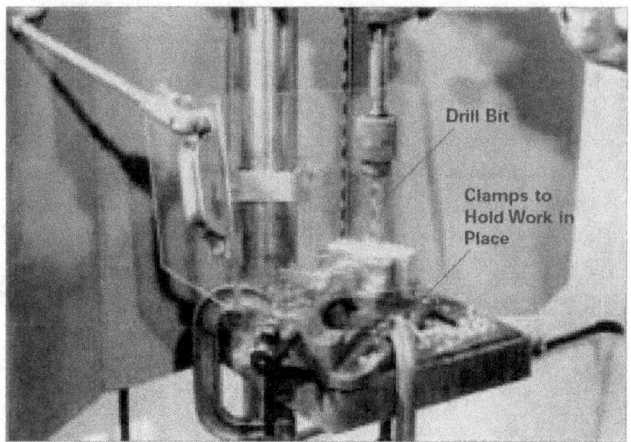

*Figure 40* Drill Press with a Transparent Drill Shield

Amputations typically occur when the operator's gloves, loose-fitting clothing, or jewelry become entangled in the rotating drill bit. Here are some other causes of drill press-related amputations:

- Inadequately guarding points of operation or power-transmission (such as belt and pulleys) devices;
- Removing a part from a drill press while wearing gloves;
- Making adjustments to the drill press, such as setting the depth, securing the material to the drill press bed, and repositioning the wood or metal, while the drill bit is still rotating;
- Changing the drill bit with the operating control unprotected so that a falling object or otherwise bumping the switch can accidentally start up the press spindle and tool assembly;
- Performing servicing and maintenance activities, such as changing pulleys and belts, without de-energizing and locking/taging out the drill press.

### Case History #20

A mechanic amputated the first joints of his left index and middle fingers while changing the belt position on a multi-pulley drill press. While the mechanic was pulling the belt on, it suddenly went around the outside pulley, pulling the mechanic's fingers through the nip point.

## Safeguarding and Other Controls for Drill Presses

For drill presses, you must be protected from the rotating chuck and swarf that is produced by the drill bit. Guarding at the point-of-operation is difficult because of the nature of the drilling press. The following primary safeguarding methods can be installed to guard the operator and other employees from rotating parts, flying chips, and cuttings:

- Specifically designed shields can be attached to the quill and used to guard this area. For example, telescopic shielding that retracts as the drill bit contacts the piece or a more universal-type shield can be applied.
- Automatic machines and high-production machines could have enclosures designed and installed to guard the employee from the entire drilling operation.
- Install guarding over the motor, belts, and pulleys.
- Install an adjustable guard to cover the unused portion of the bit and chuck above the material being worked.

The following are some secondary safeguarding methods, work practices, and complementary equipment that may be used to supplement primary safeguarding or alone or in combination when primary safeguarding methods are not feasible:

- Automatic machines and high-production machines could use barricades to separate the employee from the entire drilling operation.
- Develop and implement safe work (operating) practices, such as removing the chuck immediately after each use, for drill press operations and conduct periodic inspections to ensure compliance.
- Train and supervise all operators until they can work safely on their own.
- Use the drill press only for its intended purposes.

- Instruct employees not to wear gloves, jewelry, or loose-fitting clothing while operating a drill press and to secure long hair in a net or cap.
- Make sure that operators secure material to the drill press bed with clamps (work-holding equipment) before drilling, so that the material will not spin and strike the operator. The operator should not manually secure the work to the drill press bed while drilling holes.
- Do not adjust the drill press while the drill bit is still rotating.
- Replace projecting chucks and set screws with non-projecting safety-bit chucks and set screws.
- Cover operator controls so that the drill press cannot be turned on accidentally.
- Shut off the drill press when not in use or when left unattended for any period of time.
- Perform servicing and maintenance under an energy control program in accordance with the *Control of hazardous energy (lockout/tagout)*, 29 CFR 1910.147, standard.

### Minor Servicing

At times, OSHA recognizes that some minor servicing may have to be performed during normal production operations, so a lockout/tagout exception is allowed. See the 29 CFR 1910.147(a)(2)(ii) Note, for details. For example, minor drill press tool changes and adjustments may be performed without lockout/tagout if the machine's electrical disconnect or control (on/off) switches control all the hazardous energy and are: 1) properly designed and applied in accordance with good engineering practice; 2) placed in an off (open) position; and 3) under the exclusive control of the employee performing the minor servicing task.

Source: 29 CFR 1910.147(a)(2)(ii) Note.

### Cord- and Plug-connected Electric Equipment

The OSHA LOTO standard would not apply when employees are performing servicing and maintenance work on a cord- and plug-connected drill press if the press is unplugged and the plug is in the exclusive control of the employee performing the task. The employee would be able to control the press from being energized by controlling the attachment plug.

Source: 29 CFR 1910.147(a)(2)(ii)(A).

## Hazards of Milling Machines

Electric milling machines cut metal using a rotating cutting device called a milling cutter. These machines cut flat surfaces, angles, slots, grooves, shoulders, inclined surfaces, dovetails, and recessed cuts. Cutters of different sizes and shapes are available for a wide variety of milling operations.

Milling machines include knee-and-column machines, bed-type or manufacturing machines, and special milling machines designed for special applications. Typical milling operations consist of selecting and installing the appropriate milling cutter, loading a work-piece on the milling table, controlling the table movement to feed the part against the rotating milling cutter, and callipering or measuring the part. (See *Figure 41*.)

*Figure 41* Bed Mill

Some frequent causes of amputation from milling machines include:

- Loading or unloading parts and callipering or measuring the milled part while the cutter is still rotating;
- Operating milling machines with the safety door selector switch on bypass;
- Inspecting the milling machine gearbox with the machine still operating;
- Manually checking the machine for loose gears (by removing the gearbox cover) while computerized cutting software program was operating;
- Performing servicing and maintenance activities such as setting up the machine, changing and lubricating parts, clearing jams, and removing excess oil, chips, fines, turnings, or particles either while the milling machine is stopped but still energized, or while the cutter is still rotating; and
- Getting jewelry or loose-fitting clothing entangled in the rotating cutter.

### Case History #22
While replacing parts on a horizontal milling machine, an employee shut off the machine, which put the revolving cutter in a neutral position. The employee, however, did not disengage the clutch to stop the cutter and proceeded to replace parts while the cutter was still moving. He amputated three fingers.

## Safeguarding and Other Controls for Milling Machines

The following primary safeguarding methods will help protect you from point-of-operation and other milling machine hazard areas:

- Install guards (fixed, movable, and interlocked) that enclose the milling cutter's point-of-operation;
- Install properly applied safeguarding devices, such as presence-sensing devices and two-hand control methods;
- Install guards around the machine's power transmission components (such as drive mechanisms).

The following are some secondary safeguarding methods, work practices, and complementary equipment that may be used to supplement primary safeguarding or alone or in combination when primary safeguarding methods are not feasible:

- Use other safeguarding devices such as splash shields, chip shields, or barriers if they provide effective protection to the operator and when it is impractical to guard cutters without interfering with normal production operations or creating a more hazardous situation.
- Install awareness devices, such as barriers and warning signs, around the milling table.
- Instruct operators not to use a jig or vise (work-holding equipment) that prevents the point of operation guard from being adjusted appropriately.
- Develop and implement safe (operating) work procedures for machine operators, such as safe work procedures for installing and using fixtures and tooling.
- Instruct operators to place the jig or vise locking arrangement so that force must be exerted away from the cutter.

- Ensure that all operators receive appropriate safe work procedure training by experienced operators until they can work safely on their own.
- Instruct operators to move the work-holding device back to a safe distance when loading or unloading parts and callipering or measuring the work and not to perform these activities while the cutter is still rotating unless the cutter is adequately guarded.
- Instruct employees not to wear gloves, jewelry, or loose-fitting clothing while operating a milling machine and to secure long hair in a net or cap.
- Prohibit operators from reaching around the cutter or hob to remove chips while the machine is in motion or not locked or tagged out.
- Conduct periodic inspections to ensure compliance.
- Perform servicing and maintenance under an energy control program in accordance with the *Control of hazardous energy (lockout/tagout)*, 29 CFR 1910.147, standard.

## Hazards of Grinding Machines

Grinding machines primarily alter the size, shape, and surface finish of metal by placing a work-piece against a rotating abrasive surface or wheel. Grinding machines may also be used for grinding glass, ceramics, plastics, and rubber.

Examples of grinding machines include abrasive belt machines, abrasive cutoff machines, cylindrical grinders, centerless grinders, gear grinders, internal grinders, lapping machines, off-hand grinders, surface grinders, swing frame grinders, and thread grinders. (See *Figure 42*.)

*Figure 42* Horizontal Surface Grinder

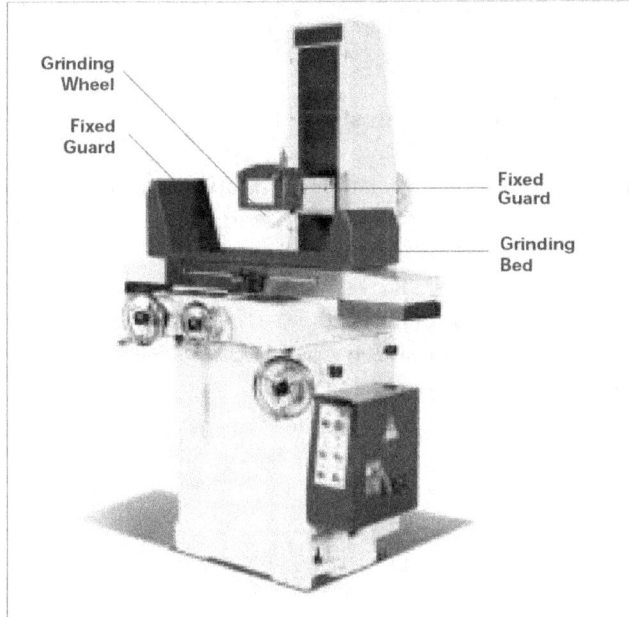

Grinding
Wheel

Fixed
Guard

Fixed
Guard

Grinding
Bed

Amputation injuries can occur when the operator's hands enter the point of operation during the following activities:

- Bypassing the grinding machine safety switch feature in order to clean the machine while it is running;
- Wearing gloves while grinding, where it is possible to have the glove get caught between the revolving disc and the table;
- Fixing a jammed grinder machine by turning the machine off, removing the blade guard and reaching into the danger area before the blades stop turning;
- Operating a grinding machine with non-functional interlocks and without the guard in place;
- Using an incorrectly adjusted or missing work rest or a poorly maintained or unbalanced abrasive wheel;
- Adjusting the work rest, balancing the wheel, cleaning the area around the abrasive wheel and loading and unloading parts or measuring parts while the abrasive wheel is still rotating;
- Attempting to stop a rotating abrasive wheel by hand.

**Case History #24**
After grinding a piece of steel on an off-hand grinder, an employee turned off the machine and tried to stop the wheel with a piece of scrap steel. His hand slipped and hit the rotating abrasive wheel, amputating the tip of his left middle finger.

**Case History #25**
An employee was operating a large surface grinder to grind a groove into a steel part in a large pump repair shop. The part was secured with a vise and placed on a magnetic table. The employee was trying to measure the groove while the table was moving back and forth beneath the grinding wheel. The safe practice, both written and customary, is to disengage the hydraulics for the table and stop the wheel before reaching in to measure or remove a part. Though experienced at operating this machine and aware of the strict rule, the employee attempted to take measurements while the table and wheel were moving and ground off part of his left index finger.

## Safeguarding and Other Controls for Grinding Machines

You can help prevent employee accidents and injuries by using primary safeguarding methods. Here are some examples:

- Install safety guards that cover the spindle end, nut, and flange projections or otherwise ensure adequate operator protection;
- Install adjustable and rigid work rests on off-hand grinding machines; and
- Install guards over power belts and drives.

The following are some secondary safeguarding methods, work practices, and complementary equipment that may be used to supplement primary safeguarding or alone or in combination when primary safeguarding methods are not feasible:

- Develop and implement safe work procedures for grinding machine operations.
- Install warning and safety instruction signs.
- Ensure that all operators receive appropriate on-the-job training and supervision until they can work safely on their own.
- Use abrasive discs and wheels that are correctly rated for the grinder's maximum operating spindle speed. The disc or wheel rating is marked on the disc or wheel in surface feet per minute.
- Inspect and sound test the grinding wheel to ensure that it is not defective, unbalanced, loose, or too small.
- Adjust the work rest to within $1/8$ inch of the wheel.
- Do not wear gloves, jewelry, or loose-fitting clothing while operating grinding machines and secure long hair in a net or cap.
- Do not adjust the guard or clean the grinding machine while the abrasive wheel is still rotating.
- Conduct periodic inspections to ensure compliance.
- Perform servicing and maintenance under an energy control program in accordance with the *Control of hazardous energy (lockout/tagout)*, 29 CFR 1910.147, standard.

### Cord- and Plug-connected Electric Equipment

The OSHA LOTO standard would not apply when employees are performing servicing and maintenance work on a cord- and plug-connected grinding machine if the grinder is unplugged and the plug is in the exclusive control of the employee performing the task. The employee would be able to control the grinder from being energized by controlling the attachment plug.

### Applicable Standards

- ANSI B7.1-1970, *Safety Code for the Use, Care and Protection of Abrasive Wheels* [incorporated by reference in 1910.94(b)(5)(i)(a), 1910.215(b)(12) and 1910.218(j)(5)].
- 29 CFR 1910.147, *Control of hazardous energy (lockout/tagout)*.
- 29 CFR 1910.215, *Abrasive wheel machinery*.
- 29 CFR 1910.219, *Mechanical power-transmission apparatus*.
- 29 CFR 1926.303, *Abrasive wheels and tools*.

### Sources of Additional Information

- OSHA Publication 3067, *Concepts and Techniques of Machine Safeguarding* (http://www.osha.gov/Publications/Mach_Safeguard/toc.html)
- OSHA *Machine Guarding eTool* (http://www.osha.gov/SLTC/etools/machineguarding/index.html)
- *OSHA Lockout/Tagout Interactive Training Program* (http://www.osha.gov/dts/osta/lototraining/index.htm)
- ANSI B7.1—2000, *Use, Care, and Protection of Abrasive Wheels.*
- ANSI B11.9—1975 (R2005), *Safety Requirements for the Construction, Care, and Use of Grinding Machines.*

## Hazards of Slitters

Slitters use rotary knives to slit flat rolled metal, plastic film, paper, plastic, foam, and rubber as well as other coiled or sheet-fed materials. Slitters range from small hand-fed paper slitters to large-scale automated metal slitters, complete with metal processing and handling units such as unwinders and rewinders. Both light and heavy gauge slitters are available. (See *Figure 43*.)

*Figure 43* Paper Slitter

Amputations often occur when clothing or body parts come in contact with slitter blades or get caught in the movement of coils and rolls. Here are some examples:

- Employees can inadvertently get their fingers and hands caught in the in-going nip points of the slitter or associated machinery such as re-winders.
- Gloves, jewelry, long hair and loose clothing can get entangled in in-going nip points or in the rotary knives of the slitter.
- Employees can suffer an amputation when clearing, adjusting, cleaning, or servicing the slitter while it is either still operating, or shut off but still plugged in (energized).

**Case History #26**
An employee was operating a precision slitting machine to slit a roll of aluminum. As the employee reached into the machine to make an adjustment because the aluminum was not being slit properly, the employee's right arm got caught in the slitter. A set of rollers pulled his arm and amputated his right thumb and forefinger.

**Case History #27**
An employee was feeding cardboard strips onto slit steel as it was being coiled on a slitter machine. While the machine was operating, the employee was placing the cardboard strips on the coils. After reaching over the steel strips, the coiled steel on the mandrel pulled his right arm into the machine and amputated it.

Source: OSHA IMIS Accident Investigation Database.

## Safeguarding and Other Controls for Slitters

The following primary safeguards may be used to protect employees from the hazardous portions of the slitter and auxiliary equipment:

- Install a fixed or adjustable point-of-operation guard to prevent inadvertent entry of body parts into a hazardous area of the slitter system.
- Install a fixed point of operation guard to cover the sides of the unwinder or rewinder to prevent an employee's hands or clothing from entering into the rollers.
- Properly applied presence-sensing devices (such as light curtains, radio-frequency devices, safety mats) may be used to control employee exposure to certain types of hazards (such as the slitter knives' point-of-operation hazard) by stopping or preventing machine system operation in the event any part of an employee's body is detected in a sensing field.
- Install fixed or interlocked guards to cover other moving parts of the machine such as the power-transmission apparatus.

The following are some secondary safeguarding methods, work practices, and complementary equipment that may be used to supplement primary safeguarding or alone or in combination when primary safeguarding methods are not feasible:

- Use awareness devices, such as an awareness barrier or fence (with an interlocking gate) and hazard warning/safety instruction signs around the perimeter of the machine to alert people of the hazard and prevent unauthorized entry.
- Awareness signals may also be used to alert you of an existing or approaching hazard as these devices issue a warning sound or provide a visible warning light.
- Restrict employee access to hazardous areas through the application of safeguarding by location techniques – such as utilizing the facility layout (walls) and equipment location (elevation) for isolation purposes.
- Develop and implement safe work procedures for machine operators and conduct periodic inspections to ensure compliance.
- Develop an operator training program to ensure that all operators are knowledgeable and proficient in the safeguarding methods and work procedures. Employees need to be supervised on a regular basis to ensure that they are following the safety program requirements.

- Perform servicing and maintenance under an energy control program in accordance with the *Control of hazardous energy (lockout/tagout)*, 29 CFR 1910.147, standard.

## Applicable Standards

- 29 CFR 1910.147, *Control of hazardous energy (lockout/tagout)*
- 29 CFR 1910.212, *General requirements for all machines*
- 29 CFR 1910.219, *Mechanical power-transmission apparatus*

## Sources of Additional Information

- OSHA Publication 3067, *Concepts and Techniques of Machine Safeguarding* (http://www.osha.gov/Publications/Mach_Safeguard/toc.html)
- OSHA *Machine Guarding eTool* (http://www.osha.gov/SLTC/etools/machineguarding/index.html)
- *OSHA Lockout/Tagout Interactive Training Program* (http://www.osha.gov/dts/osta/lototraining/index.htm)
- ANSI B11.14—1996, *Coil Slitting Machines Safety Requirements for Construction, Care and Use*

# OSHA Assistance

OSHA can provide extensive help through a variety of programs, including technical assistance about effective safety and health programs, state plans, workplace consultations, voluntary protection programs, strategic partnerships, training and education, and more. An overall commitment to workplace safety and health can add value to your business, to your workplace, and to your life.

## Safety and Health Program Management Guidelines

Effective management of employee safety and health protection is a decisive factor in reducing the extent and severity of work-related injuries and illnesses and their related costs. In fact, an effective safety and health program forms the basis of good employee protection and can save time and money (about $4 for every dollar spent) and increase productivity and reduce employee injuries, illnesses, and related workers' compensation costs.

To assist employers and employees in developing effective safety and health programs, OSHA published recommended Safety and Health Program Management Guidelines (54 Federal Register (16): 3904-3916, January 26, 1989). These voluntary guidelines can be applied to all places of employment covered by OSHA.

The guidelines identify four general elements critical to the development of a successful safety and health management system:

- Management leadership and employee involvement,
- Worksite analysis,
- Hazard prevention and control, and
- Safety and health training.

The guidelines recommend specific actions, under each of these general elements, to achieve an effective safety and health program. The Federal Register notice is available online at www.osha.gov.

## State Programs

The Occupational Safety and Health Act of 1970 (OSH Act) encourages states to develop and operate their own job safety and health plans. OSHA approves and monitors these plans. Twenty-four states, Puerto Rico and the Virgin Islands currently operate approved state plans: 22 cover both private and public (state and local government) employment; Connecticut, New Jersey, New York and the Virgin Islands cover the public sector only. States and territories with their own OSHA-approved occupational safety and health plans must adopt standards identical to, or at least as effective as, the Federal OSHA standards.

## Consultation Services

Consultation assistance is available on request to employers who want help in establishing and maintaining a safe and healthful workplace. Largely funded by OSHA, the service is provided at no cost to the employer. Primarily developed for smaller employers with more hazardous operations, the consultation service is delivered by state governments employing professional safety and health consultants. Comprehensive assistance includes an appraisal of all mechanical systems, work practices, and occupational safety and health hazards of the workplace and all aspects of the employer's present job safety and health program. In addition, the service offers assistance to employers in developing and implementing an effective safety and health program. No penalties are proposed or citations issued for hazards identified by the consultant. OSHA provides consultation assistance to the employer with the assurance that his or her name and firm and any information about the workplace will not be routinely reported to OSHA enforcement staff.

Under the consultation program, certain exemplary employers may request participation in OSHA's Safety and Health Achievement Recognition Program (SHARP). Eligibility for participation in SHARP includes receiving a comprehensive consultation visit, demonstrating exemplary achievements in workplace safety and health by abating all identified hazards, and developing an excellent safety and health program.

Employers accepted into SHARP may receive an exemption from programmed inspections (not complaint or accident investigation inspections) for a period of 1 year. For more information concerning consultation assistance, see OSHA's website at www.osha.gov.

## Voluntary Protection Programs (VPP)

Voluntary Protection Programs and on-site consultation services, when coupled with an effective enforcement program, expand employee protection to help meet the goals of the OSH Act. The VPPs motivate others to achieve excellent safety and health results in the same outstanding way as they establish a cooperative relationship between employers, employees, and OSHA.

For additional information on VPP and how to apply, contact the OSHA regional offices listed at the end of this publication.

## Strategic Partnership Program

OSHA's Strategic Partnership Program, the newest member of OSHA's cooperative programs, helps encourage, assist, and recognize the efforts of partners to eliminate serious workplace hazards and achieve a high level of employee safety and health. Whereas OSHA's Consultation Program and VPP entail one-on-one relationships between OSHA and individual worksites, most strategic partnerships seek to have a broader impact by building cooperative relationships with groups of employers and employees. These partnerships are voluntary, cooperative relationships between OSHA, employers, employee representatives, and others (e.g., trade unions, trade and professional associations, universities, and other government agencies).

For more information on this and other cooperative programs, contact your nearest OSHA office, or visit OSHA's website at www.osha.gov.

### Alliance Program

The Alliance Program enables organizations committed to workplace safety and health to collaborate with OSHA to prevent injuries and illnesses in the workplace. OSHA and the Alliance participants work together to reach out to, educate, and lead the nation's employers and their employees in improving and advancing workplace safety and health.

Groups that can form an Alliance with OSHA include employers, labor unions, trade or professional groups, educational institutions and government agencies. In some cases, organizations may be building on existing relationships with OSHA that were developed through other cooperative programs.

There are few formal program requirements for Alliances and the agreements do not include an enforcement component. However, OSHA and the participating organizations must define, implement, and meet a set of short- and long-term goals that fall into three categories: training and education; outreach and communication; and promotion of the national dialogue on workplace safety and health.

### OSHA Training and Education

OSHA area offices offer a variety of information services, such as compliance assistance, technical advice, publications, audiovisual aids and speakers for special engagements. OSHA's Training Institute in Arlington Heights, IL, provides basic and advanced courses in safety and health for Federal and state compliance officers, state consultants, Federal agency personnel, and private sector employers, employees, and their representatives.

The OSHA Training Institute also has established OSHA Training Institute Education Centers to address the increased demand for its courses from the private sector and from other federal agencies. These centers are nonprofit colleges, universities, and other organizations that have been selected after a competition for participation in the program.

OSHA also provides funds to nonprofit organizations, through grants, to conduct workplace training and education in subjects where OSHA believes there is a lack of workplace training. Grants are awarded annually. Grant recipients are expected to contribute 20 percent of the total grant cost.

For more information on grants, training, and education, contact the OSHA Training Institute, Office of Training and Education, 2020 South Arlington Road, Arlington Heights, IL 60005, (847) 297-4810, or see *Outreach* on OSHA's website at www.osha.gov. For further information on any OSHA program, contact your nearest OSHA regional office listed at the end of this publication.

### Information Available Electronically

OSHA has a variety of materials and tools available on its website at www.osha.gov. These include electronic compliance assistance tools, such as Safety and Health Topics, eTools, Expert Advisors; regulations, directives and publications; videos and other information for employers and employees. OSHA's software programs and compliance assistance tools walk you through challenging safety and health issues and common problems to find the best solutions for your workplace.

A wide variety of OSHA materials, including standards, interpretations, directives and more can be purchased on CD-ROM from the U.S. Government Printing Office, Superintendent of Documents, toll-free phone (866) 512-1800.

### OSHA Publications

OSHA has an extensive publications program. For a listing of free or sales items, visit OSHA's website at www.osha.gov or contact the OSHA Publications Office, U.S. Department of Labor, 200 Constitution Avenue, NW, N-3101, Washington, DC 20210: Telephone (202) 693-1888 or fax to (202) 693-2498.

### Contacting OSHA

To report an emergency, file a complaint, or seek OSHA advice, assistance, or products, call (800) 321-OSHA or contact your nearest OSHA Regional or Area office listed at the end of this publication. The teletypewriter (TTY) number is (877) 889-5627.

Written correspondence can be mailed to the nearest OSHA Regional or Area Office listed at the end of this publication or to OSHA's national office at: U.S. Department of Labor, Occupational Safety and Health Administration, 200 Constitution Avenue, N.W., Washington, DC 20210.

By visiting OSHA's website at www.osha.gov, you can also:
- file a complaint online,
- submit general inquiries about workplace safety and health electronically, and
- find more information about OSHA and occupational safety and health.

# References

## American National Standards Institute

- ANSI B5.52M-1980 (R1994), *Presses, General Purpose, Single Point, Gap Type, Mechanical Power (Metric)*
- ANSI B5.37—1970 (R1994), *External Cylindrical Grinding Machines—Centerless*
- ANSI B5.42—198 (R1994), *External Cylindrical Grinding Machines—Universal*
- ANSI B7.1—2000, *Use, Care, and Protection of Abrasive Wheels*
- ANSI B11.1-2001, *Safety Requirements for Mechanical Power Presses*
- ANSI B11.3-2002, *Safety Requirements for the Construction, Care, and Use of Power Press Brakes*
- ANSI B11.4-2003, *Safety Requirements for Construction, Care, and Use of Shears*
- ANSI B11.8-2001, *Safety Requirements for Manual Milling, Drilling and Boring Machines with or without Automatic Control*
- ANSI B11.9—1975 (R2005), *Safety Requirements for the Construction, Care, and Use of Grinding Machines*
- ANSI B11.12-1996, *Safety Requirements for Construction, Care, and Use of Roll-Forming and Roll-Bending Machines*
- ANSI B11.14—1996, *Coil Slitting Machines Safety Requirements for Construction, Care and Use*
- ANSI B11.19-2003, *Performance Criteria for Safeguarding*
- ANSI B20.1-57, *Safety Code for Conveyors, Cableways, and Related Equipment* [incorporated by reference in 1926.555(a)(8)]
- ANSI B65.1-2005, *Safety Standard—Printing Press Systems*
- ANSI B65.2-2005, *Binding and Finishing Systems*
- ANSI O1.1-2004, *Safety Requirements for Woodworking Machinery*

## American National Standards Institute/ Conveyor Equipment Manufacturers Association

- ANSI/CEMA 350-2003, *Screw Conveyors for Bulk Material*
- ANSI/CEMA 401-2003, *Unit Handling Conveyors—Roller Conveyors—Non-powered*
- ANSI/CEMA 402-2003, *Unit Handling Conveyors—Belt Conveyors*
- ANSI/CEMA 403-2003, *Unit Handling Conveyors—Belt Driven Live Roller Conveyors*
- ANSI/CEMA 404-2003, *Unit Handling Conveyors—Chain Driven Live Roller Conveyors*
- ANSI/CEMA 405-2003, *Unit Handling Conveyors—Slat Conveyors*
- ANSI/CEMA 406-2003, *Unit Handling Conveyors—Line-shaft Driven Live Roller Conveyors*

## American National Standards Institute/ American Society of Mechanical Engineers

- ANSI/ASME B20.1-2003, *Safety Standard for Conveyors and Related Equipment*

## National Institute for Occupational Safety and Health

- NIOSH Current Intelligence Bulletin (CIB) 49, *Injuries and Amputations Resulting from Work with Mechanical Power Presses* (May 22, 1987)

## National Safety Council

- National Safety Council, Accident Prevention Manual for Industrial Operations: Engineering and Technology. 9th ed. Itasca, IL
- National Safety Council, Accident Prevention Manual for Business and Industry: Engineering and Technology 11th ed. Itasca, IL

## Occupational Safety and Health Administration Standards

- 29 CFR 1910.147—*Control of hazardous energy (lockout/tagout).*
- 29 CFR 1910.211—*Definitions.*
- 29 CFR 1910.212—*General requirements for all machines.*
- 29 CFR 1910.213—*Woodworking machinery requirements.*
- 29 CFR 1910.215—*Abrasive wheel machinery.*
- 29 CFR 1910.217—*Mechanical power presses.*
- 29 CFR 1910.219—*Mechanical power-transmission apparatus.*
- 29 CFR 1926.300—*General requirements.*
- 29 CFR 1926.301—*Hand tools.*
- 29 CFR 1926.302—*Power-operated hand tools.*
- 29 CFR 1926.303—*Abrasive wheels and tools.*
- 29 CFR 1926.304—*Woodworking tools.*
- 29 CFR 1926.307—*Mechanical power-transmission apparatus.*
- 29 CFR 1926.555—*Conveyors.*

## Occupational Safety and Health Administration Instructions

- OSHA Instruction CPL 03-00-003, *National Emphasis Program on Amputations*
- OSHA Instruction STD 01-12-021—29 CFR 1910.217, *Mechanical Power Presses, Clarifications* (10/30/78)
- OSHA Instruction CPL 02-01-025, *Guidelines for Point of Operation Guarding of Power Press Brakes*
- OSHA Instruction STD 01-05-019, *Control of Hazardous Energy (Lockout/Tagout)—Inspection Procedures and Interpretive Guidance*

## Occupational Safety and Health Administration Training Programs

- *OSHA's Lockout Tagout Interactive Training Program* (http://www.osha-slc.gov/dts/osta/loto-training/index.htm)

## Occupational Safety and Health Administration Publications

- OSHA Publication 3067, *Concepts and Techniques of Machine Safeguarding* (http://www.osha.gov/Publications/Mach_Safeguard/toc.html)
- OSHA Publication 3120 - *Control of Hazardous Energy (Lockout/Tagout)*
- OSHA Publication 3157 - *A Guide for Protecting Workers from Woodworking Hazards* (http://www.osha.gov/Publication/osha3157.pdf)

## Occupational Safety and Health Administration Topic Pages

- Safety and Health Topics – *Control of Hazardous Energy – Lockout/Tagout* (http://www.osha.gov/SLTC/controlhazardousenergy/index.html)
- Safety and Health Topics – *Machine Guarding* (http://www.osha.gov/SLTC/machineguarding/index.html)

# Appendix A.
# Amputation Hazards Not Covered in this Guide

The following amputation hazards and related activities are not specifically covered in detail in this document. They are either covered in other OSHA publications or specific OSHA standards. While you may find the general hazard recognition and machine guarding concepts presented in the *Recognizing Amputations Hazards and Controlling Amputation Hazards* sections of this document helpful, please refer to the applicable topic-specific resources and standards listed in the reference section of this publication for a complete discussion of these hazards.

## Amputation Hazards Associated with Saws

Saws are the top source of amputations in wholesale and retail trade and in the construction industry. Stationary saws, such as band, radial arm and table saws, account for a substantial number of amputations in the workplace. Sawing machinery used for woodworking applications is not specifically addressed in this guide.

You can find specific guidance on these saws in OSHA Publication 3157, *A Guide for Protecting Workers from Woodworking Hazards*; 29 CFR 1910.213, *Woodworking machinery requirements*; 29 CFR 1910.243, *Guarding of portable powered tools*; and 29 CFR 1926.304, *Woodworking tools*. For additional information on how to safeguard saws and implement hazardous energy control practices, you can find guidance at OSHA's Machine Guarding eTool section for Saws (http://www.osha.gov/SLTC/etools/machineguarding/saws.html) Also, the national consensus standard, ANSI O1.1-2004, *Safety Requirements for Woodworking Machinery*, may provide you with valuable information on how to prevent amputations.

## Amputation Hazards Associated with Plastics Machinery

Plastics processing machines are complex pieces of equipment that require safeguarding and a hazardous energy control program. Serious injuries, including fatalities, amputations, avulsions, burns and cuts can occur, especially during servicing and maintenance work. You can find specific guidance at OSHA's "Machine Guarding" eTool section for "Plastics Machinery" (http://www.osha.gov/SLTC/etools/machineguarding/plastics/h_injectmold.html).

## Amputation Hazards in Agriculture and Maritime Operations

Requirements for machine guarding in agriculture operations are contained in the Standards for Agriculture, 29 CFR Part 1928 Subpart D—*Safety for Agricultural Equipment*, and requirements for machine guarding in maritime operations can be found in the Shipyard Employment Standards, 29 CFR Part 1915 Subpart H—*Tools and Related Equipment*, the Marine Terminals Standard, 29 CFR Part 1917 Subpart G—*Machine Guarding*, and the Longshoring Standard, 29 CFR Part 1918 Subpart I—*General Working Conditions*.

## Additional Health and Safety Hazards

Other health and safety hazards associated with using stationary machines, but not addressed in this guide, include noise, vibration, ergonomic stresses, exposure to hazardous chemicals (e.g., metalworking fluids) and dust, electric hazards, and flying objects.

Please visit the OSHA website at www.osha.gov for more information on how to recognize and control these hazards.

# Appendix B. Amputation Hazards Associated with Other Equipment and Activities

Although machinery is associated with amputations more frequently than any other source, amputations can result from other sources. This appendix briefly identifies other equipment and activities associated with amputations:

- **Powered and Non-Powered Hand Tools.** Portable hand tools, such as saws, grinders, shears, and bolt cutters are associated with amputations in the construction, retail trade, and services industries.
- **Material Handling.** Amputations related to manual material handling tasks often result when heavy or sharp objects fall from an elevated surface or shift during transfer. Amputation often occurs when the employee attempts to limit the movement of, or damage to, material as it shifts or falls.
- **Forklifts.** Amputation hazards related to forklift operation and use include employees being trapped or pinned between the forklift and another object; struck or run over by the forklift; struck by falling or shifting loads or overturning forklifts.

- **Doors and Covers.** Amputation hazards are not limited to mechanical equipment or heavy loads. Doors also have the potential to amputate fingers. These injuries typically result when a door closes while a person's hands are in the doorjamb. Manhole covers, commercial garbage disposal covers, and tank or bin covers can also amputate fingers and toes.
- **Trash Compactors.** Many businesses use small trash compactors for reducing the volume of wastes such as cardboard. Often these compactors are not properly guarded and employees are not properly trained in their use. The majority of these amputations result from employees being struck by the ram/piston either during the initiating stroke or the return stroke. The ram/piston should be guarded if any part of an operator's body is exposed to the danger area during the operating cycle. Likewise, before reaching into any trash compactor the operator should de-energize and lock out the machine.

# Appendix C.
# OSHA Regional Offices

**Region I**
(CT,* ME, MA, NH, RI, VT*)
JFK Federal Building, Room E340
Boston, MA 02203
(617) 565-9860

**Region II**
(NJ,* NY,* PR,* VI*)
201 Varick Street, Room 670
New York, NY 10014
(212) 337-2378

**Region III**
(DE, DC, MD,* PA, VA,* WV)
The Curtis Center
170 S. Independence Mall West
Suite 740 West
Philadelphia, PA 19106-3309
(215) 861-4900

**Region IV**
(AL, FL, GA, KY,* MS, NC,* SC,* TN*)
61 Forsyth Street, SW
Atlanta, GA 30303
(404) 562-2300

**Region V**
(IL, IN,* MI,* MN,* OH, WI)
230 South Dearborn Street
Room 3244
Chicago, IL 60604
(312) 353-2220

**Region VI**
(AR, LA, NM,* OK, TX)
525 Griffin Street, Room 602
Dallas, TX 75202
(214) 767-4731 or 4736 x224

**Region VII**
(IA,* KS, MO, NE)
City Center Square
1100 Main Street, Suite 800
Kansas City, MO 64105
(816) 426-5861

**Region VIII**
(CO, MT, ND, SD, UT,* WY*)
1999 Broadway, Suite 1690
PO Box 46550
Denver, CO 80202-5716
(720) 264-6550

**Region IX**
(American Samoa, AZ,* CA,* HI,* NV,*
Northern Mariana Islands)
71 Stevenson Street, Room 420
San Francisco, CA 94105
(415) 975-4310

**Region X**
(AK,* ID, OR,* WA*)
1111 Third Avenue, Suite 715
Seattle, WA 98101-3212
(206) 553-5930

* These states and territories operate their own OSHA-approved job safety and health programs and cover state and local government employees as well as private sector employees. The Connecticut, New Jersey, New York and Virgin Islands plans cover public employees only. States with approved programs must have standards that are identical to, or at least as effective as, the Federal standards.

**Note:** To get contact information for OSHA Area Offices, OSHA-approved State Plans and OSHA Consultation Projects, please visit us online at www.osha.gov or call us at 1-800-321-OSHA.